Lioness: My Fighting Spirit

Silvana Ghoussain

Lioness: My Fighting Spirit

Silvana Ghoussain

DoctorZed
Publishing
www.doctorzed.com

Copyright © 2022 by Silvana Ghoussain

All rights reserved. No part of this book may be used or reproduced by any means, graphic, electronic, or mechanical, including photocopying, recording, taping or by any information storage retrieval system without the written permission of the publisher except in the case of brief quotations embodied in critical articles and reviews.

Updated and revised second edition published 2022 by
DoctorZed Publishing

DoctorZed Publishing books may be ordered through booksellers or:

DoctorZed Publishing
10 Vista Ave
Skye, South Australia 5072
www.doctorzed.com

ISBN: 978-0-6456195-0-8 (hc)
ISBN: 978-0-6456195-1-5 (sc)
ISBN: 978-0-6456195-2-2 (ebk)

A Cataloguing-in-Publication entry can be found at the National Library of Australia

Stylists image © clique
Cover image © fitlifeimages
Cover design © Scott Zarcinas

DoctorZed Publishing rev. date: 17/10/2022

Lioness: My Fighting Spirit

Some of the names in this book have been changed for privacy reasons.

To all who read this book:

I hope this book makes a difference to you, even if it's in a small way. I hope that some of these pages give you the inspiration and motivation to get out and do something for yourself. I have been inspired and influenced by many amazing people that have helped me along the road.

Just remember: do the things you want in life and take advice from others. Remember, at the end of the day it's listening to your heart and mind that will get you closer to your goals.

Never give up.

Just do it.

Laugh.

Surround yourself with people that will uplift you.

Learn something each day.

Just believe in yourself.

Take a risk.

Have faith in yourself.

It's OK to have fear; without fear we cannot succeed.

Do something for someone without expecting anything in return.

It's OK to fail, because when you get back up you're stronger and wiser.

Success comes from failures.

For many years, my heart and my mind have wanted to write about my colourful life, as parts of my story have been told to different people I have crossed paths with from around the world. I have been told so many times it should be in a book to be read by many.

Here it is finally. To my family and friends and my loving husband who have encouraged me to take that risk again and just do it …

Thank you. xx

Contents

Lioness: My Fighting Spirit	v
The Beginning	3
Getting To Know Myself	13
Discovering the World	17
Coming Home: The Change in Me	43
The Wedding: Las Vegas Style	47
Life in Las Vegas: Discovering Myself	55
The Turning Point	61
Cancer Hits, Making Me Stronger	65
Door Opens to New Opportunities	71
The Terrifying Accident: Going Home	81
Back in Australia: A Second Chance	87
Dark Times	95
Saving My Life and Competing In Ms Fitness/Ms East Coast	101
Alternative Path	107
Finding My Outlet	115
A Dangerous Relationship	117
Becoming a Boxing Coach: New Path	125
Going Into Business: The Making of Oxi Clothing	135
Vaska, Ambassador of Angels	145
Unplanned Chapter of My Life: The Unknown	151
Meeting My Future	155
Health Challenges Keep Coming	161

Looking Back: Fulfilling My Bucket List	167
IVF and Falling Pregnant: The Things Some Women Are Too Afraid to Voice	173
Sea Change	181
Fitness Journey Is Reborn	185
Remember the Important Things In Life	193
Three Simple Rules in Life	195

Lioness

The Beginning

'When the heart is happy it embraces the whole world.'

Sri Chinmoy

Do you want to get to know me? The events that have shaped my life until now, where I have come from and the way I was raised, have shaped my character and the woman I have become today.

In 1968, my dad came from Lebanon to make Australia his home. He came with his best friend, who was my godfather, and moved into a two-bedroom unit in Dulwich Hill, Sydney – sharing with another three men. It became a kind of halfway house, as I say: a central place where everyone came to eat, sleep and recharge. It was a place that would come full circle to me and I would end up living not even a block from my dad's humble beginnings.

He always knew to work hard; if you can make a living for yourself, you can get the things you want. As a nine-year-old in Lebanon, my father looked after the family shop but lost his parents at a young age. Having lived in a war-torn country, he saw many terrible things but somehow Lebanon always manages to rise up through the rubble to make its stance: a country that never gives up. Despite the different religious beliefs and fights over land, Lebanon still holds its head up high. The people there are fighters and spiritually and mentally we never give up.

My heritage has had a huge effect on my life, and I am proud to have that background. But I also had to have a voice. I am someone who stepped out of her culture to be an individual. I wasn't one for cooking, cleaning and baby making – I wanted to live and explore what life had to offer. Without spoiling the story, let's just say there was plenty of time to look after the house and be the baby maker later in life …

In 1971, my dad decided he would marry my stunning mother. He flew back to Lebanon but, like many parents, my grandmother thought Dad was not good enough for her daughter. She could not understand the reason for taking her all the way to Australia where they knew nothing about the country, its people, and had no family for support.

Mum was glamorous, with her long legs and hair that reached her bottom – she turned heads no matter where she was. She was nicknamed Bridget Bardot (the dark-headed version) after the famous actress in the 1950s and '60s. Even on her wedding day in 1971 she wore a dress that barely covered her bottom! But looking at the photo, it suited her to perfection and I could not imagine her wearing anything else.

After their marriage, my parents lived in Marrickville and a year later I was born. My father worked long hours even on weekends so that his family never went without food. Mum really did not know how she managed looking after me on her own at twenty-one years old, but she spent her time watching *Days of Our Lives* to help her learn English.

Australia was changing; more migrants were making their way into the country even as Australian soldiers were sent to fight a war in Vietnam. The government was evolving and wanted people to build and take the country to its next phase. Gough Whitlam was elected in 1972 at a time of growing disillusionment with the Vietnam War. There was much concern about Australia's place in the world and great social change. You can picture how much change the country was going through. The wave of migrants coming through, my parents with them, were really trying to understand the Australian way of life as it underwent great change itself. That change scared people.

Eventually, Dad helped Mum get a job with him in Redfern, but it only lasted three days. As there were no childcare centres back then, my parents left me with a babysitter. When they picked me up, they found me with bite marks all over my body and my nappy had not been changed all day. Dad and Mum were so upset at what had happened to me, but without a support system like we have now, they didn't know who to speak to. In the end, Dad spoke his mind to the babysitter and he vowed to work three jobs so they could live a better life without Mum having to work. My mother never worked again in her life.

The Beginning

I spent my days on the swings with Mum or Dad in the park across the road from where we lived. Looking back at the photos, it was amazing to see and capture those moments because they can never come back and I truly value spending time with loved ones.

When Dad had saved enough money to put a deposit on a house, my parents had to choose whether to move to Bondi or to a cheaper area with bigger properties and where my parents had friends. Although Mum really wanted to go to Bondi where they would be closer to the city, Dad decided we would buy in Guildford.

It was a culture shock for them moving out and not being around the people they had made friends with that spoke their tongue. Even though they had a great Lebanese community, to raise a family they needed to move. But it wasn't long before the new neighbours became close to us, regardless of my parents' background. They were good people, religious Church of England neighbours, and the man helped my parents with anything they weren't sure of. I would eventually call him Grandpa. He and his daughter who lived next door helped us to understand the Australian culture.

My brother was born in 1975, and while my mother was busy raising us Dad worked two jobs: as a textile designer operator (where he made fabric) and as a taxi driver. I remember him having to study a book to learn street names and how to get from place to place – it was a lot harder than today by far.

I was enrolled at Saint Patrick's Guildford School in 1976 where my Australian 'Grandpa' helped with the enrolment. Even though I was born and raised in this great country that my parents called home, my first language was Arabic, and so I struggled with English. I was even made to repeat kindergarten. I still remember being five years old, sitting on the ground with my head down, surrounded by kids I didn't know and a language I was struggling to understand.

Then in 1980 my dad decided it was time for us all to visit and get to know our extended family. I was finally able to meet my biological grandad (who was a detective in the Lebanese police force) and my grandma, along with Mum's seven siblings and Dad's five siblings – though one of Dad's brothers had died of heart attack at a young age. My father never recovered from the death of his older brother, and I could sometimes see it in his eyes when he would take a glimpse of his brother's photo.

I was going back to the country where my parents were born and raised. I made that journey to Lebanon as an eight-year-old with my mother and my five-year-old brother. I remember meeting my grandparents from my mum's side, as Dad's parents had died years before I was born. Drinking food and dancing, my family lived like there was no tomorrow, as they came from a country that had so much bloodshed over the years from war.

My brother Richard and I had a taste of the life: sipping a little red wine and even having a puff on a cigarette. We have photos of us in the village on my grandparents' roof, me holding a handgun and Richard holding a rifle with my mum's siblings around us. You might think this is unheard of, but when you are in a country that has to survive, guns need to be in households – though they were mostly used for hunting and clay pigeon shooting.

In Lebanon, my family had a home up in the mountains. Beirut was a very busy place, even families living in desecrated buildings still carried on with their daily lives. I never forgot seeing bombed buildings and families living in what was left of their home. I could see, even at that age, how strong these people were and I wanted to be like that: a strong fighting spirit, where you overcome your fear of life and just live it.

Well, I was given that chance one day when I was arguing with my grandmother. Eight-year-old me had enough of her because I didn't want to be told to do something. So I grabbed a handful of my grandmother's hair and dragged her screaming into the living room. I laugh now, but life has a funny way of coming back at you in full circle.

As it was, I was punished and put on the outer by the whole family and news spread around of how bad I was – my mother was so embarrassed. Even to this day, they mention what a brat I was for doing that. My mum realised how much physical strength I had for a little girl and this played on her mind for some time. My physical strength developed over the years so that I later in my life I would become a boxing coach and a body builder.

Late one afternoon, my mum grabbed my brother and me and fled with our family in a car to the mountains. I remember a lot of screaming and the ground shaking beneath us. When we got to my grandparents' house at nightfall, we watched as missiles were fired from Beirut to areas in Lebanon. I'll never forget seeing the missiles

The Beginning

take off – it was a frightening noise. I stood on my grandparents' balcony holding my brother's hand, and for the first time I felt real fear, though I didn't cry because I didn't want Mum to see that I was scared. I was told that we were at war again and mum explained that it was too dangerous for us to leave, but the mountains were a safe place for us. Just imagine the thoughts that were going through my eight-year-old mind with all that I saw and heard. Very few people ever experience anything like that and live to tell it, and I don't wish that on anyone.

We stayed in Lebanon for six months in total. Dad was frantic, thinking that we had been caught and that he could not get us home. I remember we prayed day and night, as we are Maronite Catholics and I was brought up in a very strict culture. Mum had been to a Catholic school, so we were shown how to pray and told about the bible. I had even been to Sunday school, where my Australian grandfather would have us go with his daughter to their church. From all that, I knew to pray so that we would get out of this alive: I believed in my faith.

When we finally arrived back in Australia, we resumed a normal life: Dad working long hours so I could get through primary school. I was put in an English Second Language class, as I had a problem with nouns, verbs, pronouncing words and putting words into sentences. I felt stupid – I didn't like being on the outer – I wanted to fit in, so I worked hard with my English. Dad also had us going to Arabic school on Saturdays. I could read and write in Arabic, and although looking back now I can understand what Dad was doing, back then I felt I was torn between my two cultures. I wanted to make English a priority and so I did. In grade six I was a 'colour captain' for my team, and when it came to any sporting events, I always took part. I loved sports, though Dad always said that you could not make a living in sports; he wanted us to go to university and become a doctor or a lawyer or something like that.

I was starting to rebel against Dad. He didn't like it, so I was getting beatings almost every day. This went on for most of my primary school days and even through high school until I did my HSC. It got to a point that I would go to school with a black eye or would cover up by wearing stockings in forty-degree heat due to the bruising I copped from dad using a branch instead of his belt.

I started to resent him: I thought this was normal and never spoke about it to anyone.

Don't get me wrong: he raised us well, and every Sunday Dad would take us out to a different area around Sydney to explore and show us how great a country we lived in, the great outdoors and exploring was our Sunday thing. I look back at this now and know that Dad was just scared of me not abiding by the rules and not growing up his way. He was brought up trying to support his family when he was just a young boy.

He was a man who travelled the world, dated plenty of women and in a way wanted to be his own person. Really, he went out to be independent and be his own man, making his own path.

He was starting see that I was following his footsteps; never stop your child from learning and becoming their own person. When a child is resentful or saying 'no', it's a sign of them becoming independent and developing into their own character. My father tried to shelter me for many years, maybe because I was a female and not a firstborn male. But I was going to change his thinking even if it took me years to accomplish.

I had to fight from a young age to become the woman I am today. I opened my dad's mind, to give my siblings a chance to experience what life had to offer, the doors opened for my brother and sister and Dad had to evolve with the times, or he risked losing all his family.

I do not hate him: I have learnt to deal with the past, accept it, let go and forgive. Though I never forgot, and it played a big part later in my life. Eventually, after going through my own journey, I realised that Dad only did what he knew and grew up with.

Grade six is when I rebelled the most and also when I started to feel insecure of myself – yes, at eleven years old.

One such incident was coming home from school crying, as I was genetically hairy, thanks to Dad – so hairy that I was getting picked on at school every day. My poor mum decided she could no longer see me in such a state that she decided to wax my legs. She made her own wax: it was like toffee and I would eat a little here and there because it tasted so good. If only she had known someone back then to market the wax to, she could have made an empire business! I loved her so much. She wanted us to be accepted and always put herself second, regardless of the outcome for her own needs.

Then the next thing was fitting in with my peers. I did a lot of mischievous things so that I could feel as sense of being accepted by my friends who were of Australian background. I wanted to hang around them as I wanted my English to improve and to fit in with the Australian way of life.

I learnt the hard way, through peer pressure and selfish behaviour, that my actions could have negative implications that effect other people. I was also taught a lesson that would change me and make me realise that playing pranks was not the way to go about gaining friends. My parents opened my eyes, and from that day on I knew that I should not be judgmental of anyone and to keep an open mind with what happens in life.

I went through my school years in an all-girls Catholic school in Merrylands. There you would always see different groups hanging out: all Lebanese, all Italians, the cool kids, and the list went on. I was alright when it came to studies and I also took a liking to sports, becoming an excellent sprinter, javelin thrower and also at shot-put, and I always competed in sports events at the school. Although my friends hated sports, I was not going to allow that to stop me from doing what I wanted. Peer pressure can have such an effect on decisions you make in life, regardless of age. You've just got to be strong mentally, and do things that you want to do, rather than be a sheep and follow everyone else. I wanted to lead and plot my own path. I sure did take a path, and I've never regretted anything that I've done. Even though I might have made a bad decision or two, I've always tried to look at it as my learning lesson in life and not be ashamed.

But yet again, I fell into peer pressure – though this one was a funny event. On one really hot day when I was in year nine, we decided to fill up balloons with water. I was on the second level of the building when a nun started walking up to us, as what we were doing was not permitted. I was then dared to throw the water balloon at her. I aimed at my target, and with such great precision – *bang!* A loud noise and the nun looked straight up at me, drenched from head to toe.

'Silvana, get yourself down here now!'

Everyone in the playground stopped and looked at me in disbelief. I casually walked down, fully expecting the wrath of Sister Nada. While everybody was in class, I was made to clean up the whole school, picking up papers and sweeping certain areas of the school in scorching forty-degree heat. I looked at the bright side: at least I got Sister Nada pretty good! I couldn't stop laughing, little rebel that I was.

I got my licence at sixteen years and was driving a Holden HQ – my parent's car. As I was the only one of my peers who could drive, I became the taxi driver, packing the girls in – mind you, we had seven in the car and no seat belts. I used to get them out, using me as the excuse though really to see boyfriends. I managed all the time to put myself second, even at a young age. It's only now that I'm middle-aged that I realise you should put yourself first, because no-one else is going to be there when you really need something from them.

As I got older, things with Dad got worse. It was always drilled into me: 'no boyfriends'. Our culture does not accept boyfriends, having sex and coming home pregnant. 'You will be disowned' he always said to me, though he would also always say, 'your brother is a male and it's different for him'.

'What's so different with him?' I asked.

'He cannot come home with a belly,' Dad said, 'and it's OK for him to have sex, he's male.'

I always spoke back and Dad hated it. Like I said in the beginning, I always managed to cop a beating. My poor mum could not speak against my dad at all, as it was not the thing to do in our culture to speak back to a male – especially a husband.

My views were different to his, and I hated it. Here I was being in a culture where I had to behave in a certain way because I was a female.

'Yet again, sports are not an income maker. You are going to be a fashion designer, Silvana, and that is it.' Dad would always drill this in my head and how he wanted me to launch a business with him when I came out of school, specialising in underwear garments. I remember when Dad would take my brother and me to the company where he worked. Richard and I would play hide-and-seek within the fabrics, and Dad would get me and place me on his lap and show me the designs and fabric that they would come up with for next season.

'Silvana this is what you are going to do when you leave school: fashion designing.'

How I felt, with the pressures coming from him, to do what he thought was best for me …

I graduated from high school in 1990, ironically getting a high

The Beginning

distinction in fashion design for being in the top 5% of students for that subject. I also did really well in ancient history: three units, and also three units in economics. These three subjects would come back into my life in years to come.

I was happy with what I did, and I had no plans of going into fashion design school or university. Maybe it was because I had Dad drilling into me how my life was going to be, so I wanted to go against him.

Most great leaders and business entrepreneurs did not go to university. There was no need to judge people if they went to university or not and I was going to be one of those people to make my own path.

So after high school (and after a lot of convincing), a whole lot of girls were going up to the Gold Coast. We didn't call it schoolies week back then, and it was nothing like now: we actually went and explored the area. I had been up there before, as we had extended family living in Brisbane and my parents always took us to Sea World: it was our family's favourite pastime.

You can never bring back that time, so whatever time you have, make time with the people that you love and care about. I always say that for friends who make the effort with you to catch up and call, reciprocate. It is so important to hold on to that; never waste your time on people that you are always chasing and saying that they are too busy to contact you. It is not a one-way ticket here. You learn that lesson, and it was the lesson you will see that I learnt when it came to friends.

With my heart on my sleeve, sometimes I would be taken advantage of, and people assume that being kind is a sign of weakness.

> 'Don't ever mistake my silence for ignorance, my calmness for acceptance or my kindness for weakness.'
>
> — Carson Kolholt

Little did they know that when this Leo roars, she will put up one hell of a fight before she gives you the pleasure of winning.

> 'The pessimist sees difficulty in every opportunity.
> The optimist sees the opportunity in every difficulty.'
>
> WINSTON CHURCHILL

This would be my mantra, as I saw the opportunity in the most challenging things that came my way and it was how I overcame and dealt with those challenges.

Early Days with Mum

Getting To Know Myself

'Note to self:
You gotta do this for you. This is for you. This isn't about anybody. Live for you. Honor you. Never lose sight of that.'

Brittany Josephina

I was now caught at a crossroads: while everyone else had jobs or went to university or was dating, I was stuck. Do not get me wrong: as soon as I turned sixteen, I worked part-time in a chemist in our area of Guildford and supported myself by paying my school fees and getting Austudy. My parents believed that to experience life and get things that you wanted, you needed to work hard. Nothing came on a silver platter and I'm so grateful that I was brought up so strict and to know what true values are.

It makes me sad to see people today who have everything given to them, sugar-coated or wrapped up in a cotton blanket; that people rely so much on other people to get them a job, or to be in that social group, have a car bought or even a house and rely on family and friends to get that for them. What happened to being independent, creating your own path and not worrying about what family, friends or society have to say? It's about you, and making that mark all on your own. I love people that are independent and differ from the rest – the ones that make that change whatever field they are in, the ones that take the risk and go for it and challenge the rest of us, to find the inner strength to make that mark on their own. I'm so drawn to people that are true individuals.

I was soon going to meet amazing people that would help me discover myself and slowly emotionally make me.

'I'm a stronger person, because I had to be. I'm smarter because of my mistakes, happier because of the sadness I've known, and now wiser because I learned.'

— UNKNOWN

Did it help me going to an all-girls school? Sometimes not. I wish it had been mixed, so I had a better interaction with the opposite sex. There really weren't many males around for me to socialise with, and I had parents who really did not think I could have males as friends. Having said that, I did have a boyfriend. Unknown to my parents, I started dating, so I could rebel against them. I was 16 years old and met him as we had to get two buses to get to school and funnily enough the meeting was at Guildford station.

So I could not think what I wanted to do, and it didn't help that my father was controlling with me. It was 1991, a hard year because our economy had hit a recession. I started to apply for jobs – and I'm talking about every day, going out there and going to interviews. With no luck, I had to apply for the dole. I hated it: I was embarrassed. Every week I went into Centrelink, then one day the case manager approached me with something that would help me and another client.

I was offered to apply for an apprenticeship in retail. It was the first time that they had launched a programme in NSW where the government helped young people secure study and work three days with a company, so I went to an interview for a major jewellery company. I nailed the interview and my first year's intense programme began at the Centre Point store. I was interviewed by the local paper, along with the second applicant. Against all odds with the climate that we were in, I managed to get a break. I didn't feel ashamed anymore because it was determination, and with the help of the case manager who instructed me how to present myself in an interview. I was hired in a climate where the jobless rate was very high.

They do not teach you how to transition from school to work. I do not care what anyone says, you get thrown out into the real world and soon enough you've got to survive in a world where the wolves are out in force. So staying strong and filter out the good people from the bad. This is something I was going to learn really quickly.

So I graduated from my one year apprenticeship and was promoted to become a second-in-charge at the Church Street store at Parramatta at nineteen years old. I had achieved great results from the programme: I had begun to know myself and how to interact properly with the real world. I stayed with the jewellery company for five years, saving my money as I had plans to travel. I had met a girl who worked in the menswear shop next door who wanted someone to backpack with around the world. I was all for it, though I never told my parents because I knew the outcome.

During the time in the jewellery store, where Church Street was a very busy place, it thrived with retail and corporate business; it was such a happening place I loved it and I loved going to work.

Then things got really bad. I was thrown out of home because my parents found out I had a boyfriend. My dad could not comprehend the need for a boyfriend, even though I never slept with him because of my culture and just didn't want to be on the outer with my family. My mother had managed to get me to stay with family friends for two weeks while she sorted out the matter. Apparently, I was such a disgrace that I had shamed my parents' reputation. Though at the time, I wondered why my boyfriend couldn't take me in, but he was from a Palestinian background and my parents thought that was awful – they had a thing about religion and race. If I was going to date, I had to go out with Lebanese males of the same religion and it had to lead to marriage. No pressure here at all.

I eventually moved back home, though I hated it and felt like I was living in a stranger's home. I needed to do something, so my aim was to keep saving and go overseas; I needed an outlet, and to discover myself – away from friends, family and being sheltered in a bubble. I knew there was more to life than this. I needed to find my inner peace and happiness, so I was determined to achieve my goals.

I also managed to have my first life-threatening health scare at nineteen years old. I was at work in 1992, just doing my duties like normal, then suddenly I experienced a very hot sensation come over my left leg. I lifted my skirt and saw that my leg was going black and blue from my ankle and travelling up. My gut feeling told me that I needed to leave, so I left work going to the doctor. The doctor took one look at it and said that I needed to go to hospital: I was having a blood clot. I was in shock, but the doctor said that it was a public holiday and it would be quicker for me to go to Auburn Hospital myself than have an ambulance come. So I went home first to let my mum know, and she ended up driving me. I was admitted, and it was the toughest thing to go through at nineteen years of age.

I was in hospital for a week. Going to the toilet and being bathed all happened on the bed. I was given medication to get the blood clot out. I was so lucky: the clot almost hit my lung. I was looked after by the universe, and I survived. I also realised how much my mother loved me. She would come every day to bathe me and help me go to the toilet while on the bed. There is nothing like a mother's love, and it brought me closer to my mother.

I had got the clot for being on the pill. For three months I had been taking it to help get my period on a regular cycle, for my acne and the overwhelming amount of hair on my body and my face. It was such a problem I faced. I was embarrassed that I was going through this. My parents had to be convinced that the pill was only for that and nothing else. Mind you, I never took advantage of this by sleeping with my boyfriend; I just didn't want the backlash. I was told by the doctors that I would never be able to use the pill again. The fine print on the pill packet states blood clots as a possible side effect, and I was the one percent that fell into that category.

Nearly losing my life changed my views on my life. I re-evaluated my home life, work, the friends that I had and even the boyfriend. I wanted to go and experience life and what it had to offer. I was ready for the next big thing. I was bound for abroad.

Discovering the World

'One's destination is never a place, but a new way of seeing things.'

HENRY MILLER

'I hope when you board that plane, you never come back!'
Those words never left me as I travelled that day in March 1995, twenty-one years old. My father looked at me, my backpack in one hand. My travelling friend was waiting outside. I had only given my parents two days' notice that I was going for nine months of adventure.

'How could you just go? Only sluts go and do what you're doing, and girls with no family.'

I could not answer him: I was tired of his tyranny. All I could remember as I walked outside, Mum crying, was how I grew up trying to please my father: helping him when we renovated the house, digging up the foundations, helping with brick work. I worked like a bloke – I was a tomboy. I believed my father wanted a firstborn son but instead he received a female that became her own person at a very young age.

While girls at fifteen years old were out shopping and dating or hanging out with friends, any spare time I had was helping Dad with renovations. It was what a man would do, but I did the job, though my hands would bleed and bruise as I worked – I wanted him to know that I was just as tough physically and mentally. While my brother did what normal boys of twelve did – riding his bike, playing with other kids on the street – he was eventually made to do his time working and helping with the renovations.

I walked towards my friend Tracey.

'Are you OK? What happened?' she asked. I said all is fine: I was ready for this trip, even though I was leaving my mother to cope with the harassment from my father.

First stop was New Zealand. I remember the band Pearl Jam being on our flight: they were quite rowdy on the three-hour flight.

It was funny watching them though, and they kept us all entertained. I had only ever been to Lebanon before. I looked over to Tracey who was asleep and then I drifted back to memories of 1991. I'll never forget that scary flight from hell when we hit severe turbulence.

I remember sitting next to a cop, who worked at Kings Cross Station and was going to Lebanon for the first time. He was a bit older than me and as we hit turbulence, to the point where people fell out of their seats because they didn't listen to the flight attendants about fastening seat belts, he held my hand. He had fear in his eyes, and here is me thinking what the hell. We were told to get into the safety position. All I said was, 'Pray and it's going to be OK'. I really didn't know what to say, as everyone around me was in such a state. I saw a few ladies praying in the aisle and I knew that they were Muslims as I could understand what they were saying. I just kept looking at them: when you are in a situation like this, no matter what religion or race, it's about coming together. I knew it was going to be OK, because I had faith. As I looked outside, I could see the sun and I smiled as we were now over the mystic Sahara Desert.

The plane levelled out: we were out of the turbulence. I think the cop beside me was embarrassed that he grabbed me the way he did. I looked at him, and though no words were exchanged he knew that I was OK with him holding onto my arm so hard, and there was no need to be ashamed. Sometimes the comfort of a stranger, that little gesture, can make a difference in someone's life. No matter how small, it can have an impact on the person. I remembered this in years to come as a boxing coach: the actions that you take, the body language, it all comes full circle.

We landed at Beirut airport and met with my family again. That time, there was a lot of exploring the country. I said sorry to my grandma again for pulling her hair, back all those years ago. She laughed and said how stubborn and determined I was at such a young age.

I clearly remembered exploring with my three cousins and a friend, and how we spent the whole time on their motorbikes. I enjoyed my life. I travelled a lot with Adam, who is my cousin from my dad's side, on his bike. He took me to an area, close to the Syrian border, where I saw Baalbek, known as God of the Town. What a place. My ancient history studies came back to me. I was lost in a city that was built over 5000 years ago. Here I stood with my cousin, lost for words; this temple was high, reaching for the Gods. The Romans had built this. I looked at the structure and was amazed at the artwork and detail that went into these stones.

As we made our way back to Beirut, yet again Silvana managed to get herself into trouble. I was scolded because I could have been abducted as there was tension on the border with Syria and Lebanon. Being female I was an even bigger target, plus having an accent, and not to mention I was a risk-taker who even managed one day to have the Lebanese army downstairs from my aunt's unit, in Jounieh. She and her husband were well known for the famous sweet store called Tuscany in Jounieh, and I had managed to get on the walkie-talkie with my other cousin TJ, just for fun to see who we could get over the frequency. I managed to get a guy and he kept talking to me, until they tracked our location. I had to go downstairs with my aunty and mum and TJ to explain that I accidentally got onto the Lebanese army frequency; I was not a spy, as my family thought that they were going to take me away for questioning. I was let go, and I thank the universe above and God for letting me go on a warning!

My extended family thought I was nothing but trouble. One day when out with Grandma, Mum and my aunties, I was snapping photos of the Lebanese army because I found it so intriguing. The car was stopped and I was asked to show my passport and explain the reason why I was taking photos. My family all panicked and I was just sitting there explaining. The solider took my camera and destroyed the film in front of me, then handed my camera back. As he turned his back, two black SUVs went past with men standing out of the roofs with machine guns in hand. My grandma grabbed me and told me not say or do anything or to start snapping photos. I looked at her sheepishly, as yet again I had upset her.

As we took off, we drove past the blown-out buildings where people actually lived. You never forget how much Lebanon has taken in many years. I was lucky to be Australian–Lebanese first generation, living and having the good life. Even though I have struggled with my father, I realised that he only wanted the best for his wife and children and growing up where you had to fight and survive, I can see why he treated me the way he did. If anything, thank you Dad: you made a woman that would become very tough mentally and physically. I was going to cope with a lot that came my way and it was a way that I was able to handle things better than most people that would make me a true individual.

So my next event was going up to the mountains that really just tipped the whole family. I was in the car with my four male cousins, going to Saint Charbel-Annaya Monastery. We were stopped at a checkpoint, as there was tension and Lebanon was also occupied by the Syrian army. The officer looked in the car and asked me straight out for my passport in Arabic. I understood him, though I was being a smart arse and replied in English. I laughed out loud as he read my passport upside down.

Oh please, you're reading it like you know what you're doing, I said to myself.

He looked at me and responded with: 'What are you laughing at?' in Arabic.

'You are reading it upside down,' I said, and my cousins in the car were now getting scared.

The man looked at me again and said, 'What are you doing in a car filled with males?'

'I am with my cousins and we are going to pray and my mother said it was fine to go with them.'

I kept looking at him, while my cousin kept poking me in the leg. I got the message: stop being a smart arse.

I could see that the officer was thinking over time what to do with all of us in the car; I could see he was putting his hand on his machine gun and I kept looking at him in silence. Was it his way of putting fear in us? And then, just like that, he gave me my passport and said that I should pray more than my cousins. My cousins apologised on my behalf and then we were off again.

My time in Lebanon was greeted with knowing my roots and a few close calls – even going out and discovering ancient ruins each day. Some people from Lebanon are fair, due to the crusades coming from England; you see a lot of red hair and blondes. I was so enlightened about the history; we had been excellent traders and businesspeople, throughout the years and we could naturally sell well.

I travelled a lot with my cousin on his bike to different events because he was a camera man for LBC, one of the bigger broadcasting stations in Lebanon. I would go behind the scenes of filming or whatever news event there was.

Back in the present, Tracey was awake and I was smiling from ear to ear.

'What are you smiling about?'
'Memories Tracey. Sweet memories.'

We landed at Auckland airport, where we found ourselves in a backpackers' hostel. My time in New Zealand was amazing: we meet generous people, some of which even had us staying with them.

From there, we made our way to Hawaii and stayed for a month. Yet again, the hostel was our base. Staying in hostels was a way to see different countries on a shoestring budget and meet with people from all walks of life doing the same thing: discovering the world.

Three days into our stay, we were out one night and met two navy guys stationed at Pearl Harbor. They were really nice, genuine guys, they showed us around the island and we even got to travel with them and a few others on their motorbikes, to see a bit more of Hawaii.

We were shown where USS Arizona had sunk, where a memorial has been built over the ship. It was a weird feeling knowing that the men that died that day were still in the ship below. I looked above and pictured the Imperial Japanese Navy bombing Pearl Harbor. They had no chance. The loss that day was massive, and I am forever grateful for the men and women that have fought and died for their country and the military back home that are now serving for theirs. My respect grew much more that day. A few times we were taken onto their base when they had movie nights in one of their halls, where families gathered and took time out to enjoy the moments.

As Tracey and I continued our journey – meeting people, going to bars, dancing – something stood out to me: no matter the race, religion or colour you are, we hung out together, and that is something that I needed more of. I was coming out of my shell, being surrounded by the culture I grew up in.

Do not get me wrong: I am proud of my background, but I needed to see how the rest of the world lived and I took in each day and woke up grateful for the journey that I was on.

We had a small group of mixed internationals at different age groups now, trying different things and exploring, whether it was snorkelling, or swimming in the rivers. One event that stood out was the North Shore surf competition, which was surfing the pipeline. We had stumbled that day on to this amazing beach, with waves still to this day I have not seen in my life. There were so many people on the beach we asked what all this was, and we were told this is one of the biggest events for surfing in the USA. I sat in awe, watching these men surf and take on Mother Nature in its force; I was yet again exposed to things I just would have not been able to do at home, due to where I lived, my friends and culture.

We stayed, as we all wanted to see the amazing sunset that everyone talked about. The sun was something I took in, with its large colourful shades of red and orange that glistened on the waves below and took everyone's breath away. With people snapping away with their cameras, this was amazing. Here I was taking in the beautiful beauty and was sharing it with people I hardly knew and in a country that was new to me.

Our next journey was to California. I had heard so much about this place, and we ended up exploring and staying at Anaheim, seeing the magical world of Disneyland. It was the very same day that the Oklahoma bombing happened: 19 April 1995. As we did not have mobiles, my mother was just so scared. Tracey and I contacted family to ensure them that we were safe and sound. It was a pretty big thing to happen: 168 people died that day and 500 more were injured.

Was it the beginnings of what was to come years later with terrorist attacks? The mood for months was very despairing.

Our path changed: just like that, we decided we would go to Las Vegas. Although Tracey was getting a very bad migraine, we boarded a bus that would take us three hours to get there.

We arrived in the afternoon. It was amazing seeing this city in the middle of the desert. We stopped on the famous strip and found a drugstore to get headache tablets for Tracey. We arrived at the wrong time and wrong place though, as within five minutes, a man stormed in to hold-up the store. We had a look over the shelves, was this for real? Tracey thought this was all a big joke and kept laughing.

'Tracey, this is not a joke. This chemist is being held up, stop laughing.'

The man, as I remember, was high. He was walking up and down the aisles and demanding drugs, waving around what looked like a gun. Then he demanded the doors close at the front of the shop.

'No-one is leaving!' he screamed.

I told myself, *OK Silvana keep calm and try to get Tracey to stop laughing.*

By now we were crouched on the ground, as we were the only ones near the entry. I could see that part of the strip was closed down and that a helicopter was landing on the road. I saw a police officer crouching down near the entry and he could see Tracey and me; he was assuring us that yes everything was going to be fine. He held a shot gun in his hand. I turned to Tracey, who by now was snapping photos of the police officer.

'You are unbelievable! This is a serious situation Tracey.' I took the camera out of her hand, trying to be quiet. I still have those photos Tracey took; she was very brave to do what she did.

Tracey realised after seeing more officers outside, that this was now a very serious situation. We had been in there for a few hours: we were hostages. The man had come up to both of us and I prayed that Tracey would not open her mouth.

What do I do? I thought, *look at the ground or do I look him straight at him?*

If I looked at the ground we could be asked questions but at the same time I did not want to show that by looking at him I was cocky. My gut said to look at him and to be as calm as I could be. Those few seconds that he watched us both I thought the worst, though he walked away and before you knew it – just like that – he handed himself in. He was not much older than us. Still to this day, I think about what it was that caused him to hand himself in, and that maybe seeing us just triggered him to stop what he was doing.

The police officers had him handcuffed, the paramedics had all the hostages checked and we gave our statements. I just wanted to carry on our journey, but as we turned to head down a path it was now filled with reporters coming up to us. There were bystanders everywhere. I just wanted peace: I did not want to be harassed. Tracey fainted and I grabbed her, just in time.

As I grabbed her, a young man came out and helped me with her – we placed her in a corner outside the drugstore and he helped me with water. She was checked again by paramedics. I mentioned that we just needed to go to the hotel. The man, James, offered to take us back to the hotel and I accepted; this would be the start of a so-called whirlwind romance with him.

He dropped us off and I thanked him, thinking that was it and I would not see him again. He asked if Tracey was better later in the evening if we would join him at the Hard Rock Hotel. I asked for his number and said that I would contact him either way. I have always been a person that does the things I say I am going to do – whether going out with someone or duties – unless I am truly sick or there's an emergency.

I guess I thank my parents for the way we were raised with having values and being able to put ourselves in someone else's situation. I get irritated by people who are all talk and no action. There would be so many people that I would come across that will be just that: talkers.

That night, after I had called James, Tracey and I were on our way to the Hard Rock Hotel. We just wanted to move forward with what happened. I was not going to allow what happened today to affect the rest of the trip – we were just at the wrong place at the wrong time, things happen, but we are alive and well and we had our health, so be it.

We arrived to be greeted by James and his South American friend Hugo. I loved the place: the hotels in Las Vegas were huge, and everything was bigger and better. We could see a few stars scattered around at the bar.

'Wow!'

'Yes, you will see a lot of stars in Las Vegas: it is normal to see that and people respect their privacy, so they can enjoy their time without being harassed,' James told me.

So our evening went really well with the two men and I saw James again, a few days before Tracey and I took off to LA to catch up with friends we met in Orange County. When we first arrived in LA, I could not believe the hospitality of complete strangers. The couple we met were from two different sides of culture. I admired them, as against all odds they had made their relationship work.

We managed to stay with them for a few days, until we boarded a flight to our next destination, Germany, to see my uncle from my mother's side. I know when he came out to

Australia we kids did not treat him great at all. I wanted to mend that, now that I was older and a bit wiser.

So when we arrived at Bonn, I was greeted by my uncle and his wife. They never had children; that is hard thing in my culture. Even at a young age they push you to have children. 'When you grow up, you are going to get married and have children,' they say – like it's already written for you. They think that you must follow what society or culture says – well, that was not going to be my books. My story was going to be to live and to live my life how I want: if my path wanted a man and kids, well let that be.

Tracey and I settled in quite well on the banks of Bonn River where my uncle lived. Everything was so green and I could not believe that the river was the backyard. My uncle Edward pointed out across the river to the University Bonn, which he taught at; this is one of the most prestige universities in Germany. My uncle was a professor there and lectured in a variety of languages: he spoke and could read and write in eight different languages. He had been a priest in Lebanon for many years and ended up at the Vatican in Italy for a long time until he decided that he wanted something different. I was so amazed with his life and happy that he ended up finding the happiness he deserved. I still felt bad about the awful pranks I, and my brother, had played on him. Maybe it was because I never had extended family around us before and I just didn't know how to act around him. It seemed that all that was forgotten, and we enjoyed the fact that we had each other's company again, and so we stood watching the river as its calm currents moved downstream. It was a glorious afternoon and I was caught in a moment that I had never felt before.

It was time to leave Bonn and make our way to Stuttgart. After arriving at Stuttgart, we met a lovely man while we were eating in the park. We ended up befriending this gentleman, and he asked us if we wanted to stay at his home as he had to go away for a few days for work.

We were shocked he had given us the keys to his house, and he said that when we left, to leave the keys in the safe place that he showed us. What the hell – trust this guy who has given us keys to his home! So he was off and we had a beautiful home for free to stay at. We decided that we would explore the area, the cafes, the people, the vibe – all so friendly.

You could see that World War II had damaged most of the historical buildings. I pictured that time and how it would have been for them. It didn't surprise me that the people were fair with the fair skin and blonde hair and light eyes that had been passed down due the terrible reign of Hitler.

So like two little school girls, we made our journey to the fountain where people were just sitting down reading, eating and enjoying the sun. We meet an Assyrian guy who was the same age as us; for the first time, I would learn how the other people lived, as he was a refugee who had made Germany his home. We decided that we needed to be really silly and have some fun, as the temperature was rising, so we jumped in the fountain and played in the water. It felt amazing not to care and not to think about my life back home. I was a child again playing and enjoying the moment and the people that were there with me; nothing else mattered.

That evening, the three of us decided that we would all take a bottle of wine and climb up to a castle that had managed to stay standing even after World War II. It was constructed in the early eleventh century and sat high above the city. There we sat and waited for the moon to take us captive with its bright light, shining upon its city and people. It was magical, all three of us sat there in silence to enjoy the beauty that we were surrounded by, taking turns drinking out of the wine bottle. We didn't want the night to end and for the first time I was introduced to a world of underground rave night clubs. I loved the trance: the people, just in their own zone, and the laser shows that they used. It was packed, and we danced – danced till the sun rose up …

Our journey in Stuttgart came to an end, as most of our travels were with the Euro Train, buses and boats. We wanted to experience and meet different people, but we also wanted to save money and be frugal so we could experience more. Well, we had an eight hour wait before going to Italy so I laid down, away from the crowd, and slept on my backpack with my hat beside me. When I woke up, I had money sitting in the hat. Wow, they must have thought I was homeless! It was enough money to have two dinners with. The thought of being homeless came over me because subconsciously I had put myself in that position; I was grateful that I was born and raised in Australia.

Arriving in Italy, I remember staying at a hostel where we would share a room with nine other females. We found an area that used to be a church. My attention gazed up and was transfixed with the detailed paintings on the ceiling; they had dated back from the twelfth century. My mind took me back to that time and how and who would have been standing in this room. Goosebumps had come out all over my body: history was surrounding me.

We had met a few American girls and decided that we would explore Italy together. We went to the Vatican, the Coliseum and Pompeii, and in each place I took myself back to that moment in time, maybe to feel what it would have been like with the eruption of Mount Vesuvius in 79 AD. Walking the streets was hard, as you basically had to jump to each stone, so it took us a day exploring the area.

In Pompeii, we found two bodies that were facing each other. The people were caught in the poisonous volcanic lava, and the superheated gas cloud which struck Pompeii following the initial ash fall-out asphyxiated and baked any remaining people in the town. I had jumped over the fence to take the photos; I was caught in that moment looking at the bodies that were in front of me.

We also managed to go to Venice and coming back to Rome we parted ways with the American girls. That night, we met four older men who actually showed us a really good night in Rome. I remembered that pizzas and coffee were like nothing in Australia – the flavour was different: it was so much better in Italy. The men paid for everything, and I could not believe the journey that Tracey and I'd had so far: it was amazing meeting people who just wanted us to enjoy their county. No prejudice, and no religion or culture was made fun of; we all united to learn each other's ways of life. That was amazing and not everybody can experience this in their life. I was living a dream without even knowing it.

Tracey and I made our way to the Italian Riviera the next day by train. I remember that a lady had started yelling at us for sitting down; it was a packed train, and her only reason was that she wanted to sit down. Mind you, she was not much older than us and she was in perfect health. I told Tracey that we should remain seated so, to the disbelief of both us, the lady sat on Tracey. I laughed and turned to the disgruntled lady and told her to get off, though my face was a face of a smiling assassin's without fail. The lady got off Tracey and I didn't say anything after that, just looked at her. I think I was ready to put up a fight with that drama that came our way.

Tracey and I explored the coast. Amazingly, we did not have accommodation though we did spend the night on the beach in boats that were on shore and had the covers over us. The next morning as we got out the police approached us and asked us what we were doing in the boats. So, being two females, we put on the act and said we had no accommodation. We got off with a warning, but it did not matter because we were off to Athens and our journey continued by train.

We arrived in Athens, where for the first time our hostel room was shared with males. I have never experienced that before – it was weird for me. There would have been about seven people in this one room, beds not far off from each other, just enough room to get your feet planted on the floor. Too bad if someone farted in the room or even snored, though yes I copped all that and the burping competition.

While exploring the Acropolis, my ancient history knowledge from school again came into play. The Parthenon Temple was just breathtaking. For hours I walked around and took myself back to the era and yet again my mind played with imagination.

On 15 June 1995, Tracey and I laid in bed with a few others in the room as evening came. We had been drinking shots of booze and my body moved in the bed.

I called out, 'I've been moved in my bed! I think there is an earthquake somewhere!'

'Silvana, I think you're drunk. Go back to sleep.'

'No, I'm not imaging things: I did feel it,' I mumbled to myself, 'I'm tipsy, not drunk.' Then I heard Tracey vomiting on the bed.

And then it hit. We were all thrown out of our beds.

'It's an earthquake!' I called out for everyone to get outside or under a door frame. Panic had hit in the building. I grabbed Tracey and took her outside of the building, and I made sure that we were away from anything that would fall on top of us.

I'm not sure why I called out as I had never experienced anything like that before – how did I know it was an earthquake? My gut instinct came in as I have read about them before.

We were in a solemn mood the next day. We helped the hostel clean up, though we found out that twenty-six people died that night in other towns and we got hit by a magnitude of 6.1. The town of Egio was very badly damaged. I just prayed that we all realised how lucky we were to be untouched and safe.

I grew so much and became even more grateful for the things I had – even the little things, like a complete stranger doing something which made you smile. Regardless, people thought trouble followed me. It didn't: I just experienced more and took more risks than most people. It's just called life. All these life experiences can only make you stronger and more able to deal with challenges that come your way. I was going to experience a lot more and it was how I was going to handle them that would shape me into the woman I am today. I believe I had angels that were looking after me.

A few days passed, and we boarded a boat to the Greek Islands, to keep our adventures going. Our first stop was going to be Santorini, though it took us about eight hours by ferry to get there. I ended up falling so sick on the boat that I got a severe fever. The captain had seen me slumped on my backpack and mentioned that he would move me in his cabin to rest. He even got a doctor for me and gave me medication. Tracey also had a bed and the captain mentioned that when we arrived at our destination he would knock on the door so we could disembark.

When the knock came, I woke up (as it was early morning) and I felt so much better. I really must have someone looking out for me above; I thanked God and prayed quickly. I went up to the captain and gave him my little koala bear mascot and I hugged him.

'You are amazing,' I said, 'if it was not for your help, I would not have been able to get better or get off this boat. Thank you, my friend.' Then I grabbed my backpack and headed out.

We were told on the mainland that you didn't need to book, and usually there would be an old couple to greet you and you could stay with them in one of their granny flats with your own entrance and they usually would cook for you also. So as soon as we disembarked off the boat, I was drawn to a couple that were waving at me and Tracey. Tracey grabbed my hand.

'Silvana, we found our adopted grandparents while we are here!'
'You are so right Tracey.'

They were such a cute couple – not much English but hand gestures always worked. And there we were, off with Nana and Papa. I looked back as the cruise boat pulled out, and I could see the captain waving at me. I kept waving until he was just a spec.

Every morning we would wake up to find breakfast in our granny flat. Nana cooked such a great Greek breakfast and would make sure we were fed before we headed out to explore the beaches, and at night the clubs and bars. We did happen to stumble on a naked beach party that was happening, and when we walked in the middle of this, we were the odd ones out for being clothed. Tracey and I could not stop laughing and we ran from the party. It looked like it was a private function, with a few people enjoying themselves and not ashamed to be flaunting their assets.

We decided to leave the island to discover other ones, so we hopped from island to island, exploring. Greece was ancient and magical; the water was as deep blue as you could picture and watching the dolphins that swam close to the boat on some parts of our journey was breathtaking.

When our journey in Greece had come to an end, we flew to our next destination: London. We stayed there for a month, exploring the shopping, cafes and night life. Throughout this whole time, I stayed in contact with James from Las Vegas, and he would call me every few days. I thought at times it was too much; someone was fussing over me for the first time. I was happy, though I did miss him, but I had an adventure to do and I was not going to change that because there was a guy on the scene.

Yet again, we met a lovely girl who we ended up staying with. I could not believe the kindness of people that we met on our journey. Mind you, we never really booked accommodation throughout Europe, as you never know where the road would take you.

One night, our new friend Abby decided that we should go to a white party in London, so her boyfriend picked us up and we walked into a club where everyone was wearing white. This was all new to me, as my first experience had been in Germany with the underground rave club. This was the Ministry of Sound night club and the music I loved; this was me in my element.

When I'd left high school, I ended up doing a few dance gigs for dance events around the Parramatta area – without my parents knowing – and making a few dollars. At my twenty-first birthday party, no-one knew it was me until they had a closer look. Yes, I danced at my own birthday! I had a natural ability to dance, and in years to come I would use that to help with the challenges that came my way and it would be an outlet for me. So here I was in a club that was happening, and then I got offered what looked like a white pill. Abby's boyfriend offered us one each. I asked what this does, and he said that it makes you really happy. I didn't need to have a pill to make me happy and I refused.

'I can be happy without that,' I said politely and walked away to dance on the dance floor and experience the euphoria of my own natural high.

The sun was beaming bright as we left the club. I felt like a vampire that needed to be in the dark again. It had been such a great night.

We managed to travel and see some areas of England, like Cambridge and Reading, along with Brighton. I even got a ferry to France to visit my mum's brother who had just moved to his new place. I left Tracey behind for this adventure, but we would meet again in a week's time. I boarded the ferry with some crazy soccer fans, and managed to chat with a few. England was playing against France and for the life of me I didn't know who the teams were. It was quite huge, and thousands flocked to France to see this big game.

After the ferry, I boarded a train that was bound for Paris. As I got off the train, the crowd was chanting, calling out for England. I could see my uncle John through the crowd and I ran straight to him. It had been many years since I last saw him – probably when I was eight years old. He was the youngest of my mum's siblings and the one who was really bold and adventurous. I think Mum might have given him the inspiration to travel. He had worked in Africa for many years before getting a job and becoming a citizen of France and bringing his love across, who now is his wife, to make a life with his two young children. I was proud of him: he had lived in subsidised homes, in a very small apartment.

For the next few days I helped my uncle move into the dream home he had worked hard for to give his family a better life. He was a bank manager in Paris and both he and his wife showed me on a map how to use the metro and read. They mentioned that by reading it slowly, it was like English. So, for the first time, my aunty came with me and showed me how to use the metro, without asking people to help me. She mentioned that people in Paris will only talk to you in French and are not inclined to help much. I took her advice and picked up the system well. I was daunted by the fast pace of the metro system and always had a map to explore the beauty of Paris.

Though there was a side of Paris that I knew nothing of, I saw the people that had migrated from Africa, the homeless – some without limbs, on the gutter asking for money and food. There was so much of it in almost every street and it made things real. I was so grateful for what I had, happy to have the bare essentials.

My uncle and aunt had also explained to me about the gangs on some of the metro carriages: kids from five to twelve years' old pickpocketing with an older teen who was their ringleader. I had come across this and had them approach me on the train. I had my bag across my body, though my money was on my body. I just kept looking at them and as each one tried to distract me, I said 'I know what you're doing, trying to steal from me.' I saw the ringleader sitting in a corner, watching. He said something to them and I got off the train at the next stop. I wanted to get out of that situation, so I went exploring and came up to a beautiful park. I sat on the grass and felt nature beneath me. Then I noticed that there were chairs all around the park and no-one was sitting on the grass. A lady came up to me and seemed very friendly.

'You are not from Paris, as you will get a fine sitting down on the grass.'

'Are you serious?'

'Yes,' she said back in a heavy French accent.

So I moved to a chair with Alex who I just met, a complete stranger, and before long the ranger came to ask if we had tickets, so I paid for mine and Alex's – the least I could do for someone who gave me the heads-up on not getting a fine. I spent a few days with Alex exploring Paris, learning the language and teaching her English. How ironic of me, when I struggled in primary school with English and pronouncing words and putting words in proper sentences that here I was teaching someone.

It was that day that I met my uncle at Monument Champs-Élysées. On this day, the President of France, Jacques René Chirac, was in a horse and carriage. It was a huge event. He came down the street greeting the French people, and I stood in awe as the streamers and paper came out of all the windows. The street was filled with colour, and I could see just how happy the people were – proud to have a president elected. This moment I shared with my uncle, who was standing there, so proud.

Tracey joined me for another week in Paris, then from there we made our way to Amsterdam. It was a culture shock, though I loved how open they were with life. Yes, marijuana can be bought legally over the counter and you can see escorts being paraded in the shop window for sale. I was intrigued with this whole way of life. We stayed there for only a few days then boarded a train bound for Spain.

On the train we met some amazing Americans that we would travel with. A few hours into the train ride, we were greeted by the Border Police. All I saw was people throwing drugs outside the window – it was so funny to watch, as a huge amount was dumped on the tracks.

Then the police came through as we were about to enter Spain, checking for passports and seeing if we were carrying any illegal substances from Amsterdam. As the police came through, everyone went to one side of the carriage, laughing. It was like a 'hello, welcome to Spain,' as we saw a couple having sex on the grass with nothing on. We all got up and screamed out of the window, cheering them on. Yes, welcome to Spain, where even the police officers were having a laugh.

We stayed in Barcelona and from there went to Valencia, where the beaches were crystal clear and the castle Xàtiva was there on the coastline. This castle has been there since 1092. I climbed to the top and watched the beautiful coastline Valencia had to offer. From there, we made our way to the cathedral where we saw a site that took my breath away. People were dancing and laughing, and we managed to get ourselves involved and dance with the elder people of Valencia. I was having such a ball dancing to their traditional songs! After that, we were invited to sit down to the biggest dinner feast I have ever seen. I was introduced to their traditional dish paella, and was shown how to cook it on massive dishes. There was a lot of drinking red wine and eating – we even had a go later with ringing the church bells. Here I was being flung up off my feet every time that I was ringing the bell. What an amazing memorable night it was.

There was the six of us, mainly Tracey and me and the four American males we had met. We all made a decision to go to the running of the bulls, which is held in Pamplona every year from 6 to 14 July. There was a festival vibe when we arrived. They celebrate it in honour of San Fermin the patron saint of Navarra, north of Spain. It has been celebrated since 1878, though nowadays it's nothing but a partying place but the fun and joy of it all are the common ingredients.

The night before Tracey and I went to see the running of the bulls, we sat on a hill in the Old Quarters and watched them come out. I just felt a sense of sadness, as some of these bulls would meet their fate at the end of the run.

So the next day, Tracey and our American friend had positioned us behind the wooden barracks, but our other three American friends decided that they would take part in this great event. Seriously, I prayed that they would come out of this alive. The streets were lined with people wearing white and red scarfs. The streets were small and people were hanging out from the balconies and windows. We waited a few hours, and then we heard the hoofs on the pavement, the roar coming down and people running. The bulls had an almighty power, which put a bit of fear in me and I could not imagine the guys that were running — and some females had also taken part in this.

It was all over in a second, and then we waited as the finale was in the bullring where all the runners would face the bulls and meet their fate in the ring. I left; I could not watch a bull getting killed for no reason, even though it was tradition which has been in the Spanish blood for many years.

We ended up meeting up with our heroes who ran; these guys were buzzing for days to come. We decided that all six of us would go to Morocco and do something crazy and visit an untouched culture that really has not had many Westerners come through. So we left our main bags in Pamplona and headed to the coast of Gibraltar by train.

'Tracey, we have no visas to get back into Spain.'

'We do not need them.'

'Yes we do: we will be deported back to Morocco.'

'We are Australians and females; we will get through.'

'You're crazy Tracey, don't think your good looks are going to get us back into Spain!'

'Let's take a risk Silvana; life is filled with wonderful paths to take.'

I rolled my eyes knowing this was not going to end pretty at all. We got off the train and made our way with the boys to get the next boat to Morocco. Do you ever feel that sometimes you are faced with a situation and you know in your gut that it's not right? Take my advice and listen to that gut feeling.

We disembarked in Morocco at the port of Tangier. It was busy and back in 1995 females walking around in shorts really caught the attention of the local men. We stayed in a hotel which was like something out of an *Indiana Jones* movie. Even walking through to the markets where it was small and crowded, was so different – and having men looking at you, offering for you to come and eat in their restaurants and drink the Arabic coffee. I had an advantage: I could understand the language, even though the accent was very heavy and different, I still understood. This would help me out in a few challenging situations while I was there.

We stayed there for a few days and headed down the coast where we stayed in a little shack on the beach and experienced camel riding and met with a few locals. I could see as far as my vision allowed me and the sun's rays glistened on the water and sand. I was for the first time at peace and was happy with the surroundings I was in. I was aware, and thought how glad that I went against my father to experience my life. Yes, I had followed my father's footpath, as back in the day he had travelled six months on a cruise ship around the world. I was proud that I was doing something without having someone holding my hand. I was doing this on my own.

> 'By travelling we experience life, we learn and evolve. Books cannot teach you, life experiences do.'
>
> — Unknown

Our journey ended in Morocco and we boarded the train with the boys back to Spain. When we disembarked, the boys got through. When Tracey and I got to customs, we mentioned we had no visas to get back in. Customs checked our passports, which showed that there were no visas for entry to Spain from Morocco. I tried to explain they had every reason to put us on the boat back to Morocco, but the boys tried to intervene. I told them to leave us and to make their way without us, that we would figure it out.

By now, Tracey was putting on a scene and was crying and screaming. I looked at her, knowing what I had said to her before we boarded. The two custom officers picked her up and carried her onto the boat, as she would not move. *Well this is what happens,* I said to myself. The two officers looked at me and said that I was quite calm with what was happening. I was screaming on the inside: I could not believe this drama was unfolding right in front of my eyes, when we could have not gone to Morocco but no, I had to listen to Tracey.

I knew this was going to happen. Having good looks or being female is not going to get a free ticket to get into a country without a visa. So we were bound for Morocco again. Tracey had her head down the whole time and could not look at me.

'It's going to be fine, will get another way out of here; there is always a way.'

'You're not mad at me Silvana?'

'Well, yes I am mad, though I have to be calm: it's happened. Me yelling at you is not going to get us anywhere. Let's figure out how to leave Morocco.'

We went back to the hotel we had stayed at and I spoke to the reception at the desk and tried to speak Arabic, to find out how we could get visas. She said that every week on Wednesday there is a line and it's like a green card: you wait at the Spanish Embassy outside the gates and they pick the people they want to get a visa.

'Is this a joke?'

'No, not all,' she replied.

Well I took this on board: we needed to find countries that accepted Australians into their country without a visa. There was no Google back then and getting internet access was really hard. We called the Australian Embassy to see how we could leave Morocco – it was going to be an expensive flight out of there at $600 one way. It was a lot back then. I had to call Mum and ask if she could put funds in my account and I promised her that I would pay her back when I got out of there. My mother was so happy that I was unharmed and safe, though she also could not believe that we were in Morocco.

That night, we went out to clear our minds as the next day was spent trying to get the cheaper alternative to get out of Morocco. We headed to the Spanish Embassy to try to get that lucky lottery visa. We walked around with a lot of stares, me being a brunette and Tracey being blonde, we drew attention to us.

The men were out smoking the shisha pipe and drinking the Arabic coffee, and to me this was nothing new. The women were covered from head to toe; you could only see their eyes. Their children would follow a few steps behind. This shocked Tracey, but I had been exposed to this. Even though I was not Muslim, my parents educated my siblings and I about the different cultures and I had seen this while I was in Lebanon the last time, so I was not taken aback. We did not stay out too late: we went back and rested, tomorrow was a new day. During the day, we saw men sitting around chatting, drinking coffee and smoking, without their woman and children, and I wondered what they did for a living. There were so many males during the day, just socialising.

When we got to the Spanish Embassy, there was a line; people were everywhere, screaming and waving their paperwork to get picked as they held onto the massive fences that towered above them. Tracey grabbed her passport and squeezed in, doing the same. Well, she had a better chance of being picked because she was fair. I stood back and looked at the hundreds of people that wanted a better life: was this really happening? It was all over in an hour and Tracey came out all upset.

'Plan B: I say we fly to Belgium.' So we went back and booked our flight to Belgium in a few days' time – we were getting out of here.

I developed a very bad infection that made my foot swell up and develop massive cysts on the bottom. I had to have a doctor come to look at it. I could not walk and didn't even know how I gotten this.

'Have you been walking around barefoot?' the doctor asked.

'Yes,' I said, and he said that might explain it. I told the doctor that we were flying the next day and they had to let me on the flight.

So the day came and my foot was bandaged. I could barely put any pressure on my right foot. The airline staff member saw me and asked if we wanted to board first, I acknowledged him in Arabic and he helped me. His name was Ahmad. He was happy that I could speak and understand him – and even a bigger thrill that I was Australian. So I was hobbling on board and he said that we could sit in the first class section.

'I do not want to get you in trouble.'

'Not at all. I heard what happened with you and being deported and trying to get a visa to get into Spain.'

I could not believe what I was hearing. 'How did you find out?'

'Word travels, Silvana; Tangier is a very small place.'

'We will make sure that this flight is a pleasant one for both of you.'

'You are so nice Ahmad, thank you; I am truly grateful for your hospitality.'

A few hours into our flight I was woken up by Ahmad but I did manage to get a bit of a shut eye at least.

'We are almost here at Belgium. The captain would like you to be sitting in the cockpit with him and experience the landing with your friend.'

'Ahmad, I cannot believe how much you have gone out of your way for us!'

So there we were in the cockpit, and the crew were thrilled that I could chat to them in Arabic.

Seeing all the controls and them chatting with traffic control, I was amazed: there is so much to do and they have the responsibility of the plane and passengers – including the staff. These days, because of terror attacks and 9/11, a passenger in the cockpit is unheard of and is a security breach. But back then, we had the most amazing experience, being able to see Belgium airport and going down for the landing.

It was a smooth landing and Tracey and I clapped. Everything that we experienced back in Morocco with the visas had gone out the window. This was a totally unbelieve experience and the staff were so pleasant on this airline that I was ever so proud of my heritage. We thanked everyone and I had the privilege to keep in contact with Ahmad for a few years after that, though we lost contact eventually. I was blessed to come across a person who made that part of our journey memorable.

> 'I don't know where I am going from here but I promise you it will not be boring.'
>
> —David Bowie

We got off the plane with no money and just the clothes on our back and our little bags with our toiletries.

Our plan was to get to Paris and freshen up at my uncle's place, then go to Spain to get our bags from Pamplona and fly to England, where Tracey would stay and I would head back to Las Vegas; James had asked for me to stay a few months with him, which I agreed to. So with no money, we boarded a train to Paris and I jumped over the barrier with my sore foot. I didn't care: I was in survival mode. It took us a few hours on the slow train to get there, then I had to remember how to get to my uncle's place again. I pictured it in my mind. I jumped again over the barracks at Paris and walked to my uncle's place. I was so happy that I remembered how to get there, and when my aunty opened the door, both Tracey and I were so exhausted. I was happy: what an adventure to get here! My aunty was in shock and could not believe how we got there with no money and were able to remember how to get there. My uncle had come back from work in disbelief.

We showered, ate then slept, ready for the travel back to Spain the next day.

Uncle had given me just enough money for the trip to Spain and then off we went on our way, getting our bags from the station in Pamplona and then taking our flight to England. I said my goodbyes to Tracey and arranged that she would meet up with me a month later in Las Vegas.

Staying with James was an adventure in itself. I have never met anyone who liked to drink so much. I was never around people who partied hard. It was like: live today and worry about tomorrow when it came. I was staying in Green Valley in a two-bedroomed apartment, which he shared with his flatmate Carlos.

Carlos' past was a very tragic one. I was meeting people that I would never have been exposed to back at home. I was glad that I was meeting people from all walks of life. I have always been one to mix with anyone and never judge a book by its cover, as we all have our stories and we all have challenges – some more so than others. James had told me that Carlos was stabbed multiple times by his dad, while he was asleep. He woke up to find his father towering over him in bed. His father managed to kill his sister and mother, stabbing them to death, and then turned on Carlos. It was a miracle that Carlos survived and tackled the knife from his father. His father managed to flee and go to his workplace, Caesars Palace on The Strip. He went up to the roof where he jumped off, ending his life.

'James, is this a joke?'

'No Silvana, it's not. It really happened.'

Carlos was so calm and always went out of his way to help, regardless of what happened to him in his teenage years. That never left me, and it reminded me that challenges can be meet head-on, and it shows that we can deal with them and it makes us stronger each time. Carlos was my reminder that every time I came up against a challenge, it was going to be alright.

So when Carlos was left an inheritance from his father, he had family and friends that came out of the woodwork and took advantage of all that and wiped him clean. I was devastated to hear this story, knowing he was such a good person who wanted to help others. I am in favour of helping others. Although, as I grew older, I was taken advantage of for helping the wrong people too. There are people in this world that are out to take every bit of energy out of you, and even though you do not ask for anything in return, they just keep on taking and taking. You just have to draw the line when you know that they have just been taking advantage. Negative energy is never good to have around you and some people are constantly inclined to be that way. It just brings you down and you end up being in a negative mood.

It's a good idea to always surround yourself with people that want you to be successful and want you to be happy in life. Being around people who are jealous and do not want to see you succeed can be very dangerous and that is when you need to break those ties. Some people come into your life, and even though it's a toxic friendship, there is a lesson to be learnt. There are also people that stay in your life for a long time because you value the loyalty and friendship they offer, and it's just them – the real them.

As I grew older, I must say, my friendships kept changing and I always had different circles of friends, whether they be the married ones, the ones with families, the party ones, the business networking ones and the fitness ones. My father always said to me, 'you will only have one or two friends that will always be there for you', he was right. Being such a social butterfly and networking through my work, I can still only count on one hand the true friendships I have.

As I am in my fifties, I'm actually happy with the close-knit friends I have. Too much drama can come when you have plenty of people in your life, and as you grow older you have no time for the dramas. Life is too short and I have, on a few occasions, cut ties with people who I thought were friends but who had mistreated that trust. Yes, I can be tough, and I am only looking after my own wellbeing. I learnt the hard way that by putting your heart on your sleeve, you can be taken advantage of, and that you've just got draw the line with people.

James, Carlos and Stephanie (who was at the time Carlos' girlfriend) were always hanging out together with me. There were many special moments - like standing up in the back seat of James' Wrangler and having your hair blown back. The drive at night was amazing, the moon was bright as it sat ahead of us and it felt like the four of us were forever chasing the moon. It was such a beautiful night. We got to Lake Mead and decided that we all had to swim – who cares if we were all dressed? We all went in, just being stupid.

After swimming in Lake Mead we went over to James' friend's house and caught up, even though were still a bit wet. I believe your attitude and the law of attraction attracts the things you like, such as the amazing person I met, named Bob. I was introduced to him; he was a former astronaut who had flown to space. I was intrigued about how he had got into NASA and how he ended up on a space shuttle. He explained his journey, when he saw Earth from space, and also the re-entry to Earth. I was at a party when I had come across the great man – like I mentioned before, these were the sorts of people I would not have come across back home. My energy was bubbly and happy, and by being in that space, you too can open the doors to great opportunities, if you are able to see them.

That evening came to a close and I was sitting on James' bed. It was a week before I was going home. He came out of the toilet and looked at me. 'Would you marry me Silvana?'

'Are you joking James?'

'No.'

Well this is romantic, I thought to myself. Here I was, sitting on the bed, and James just came out of the toilet and said it so casually.

Well, I said yes, and that was that.

The next day, we went over to his parents' house and announced our engagement. Our flatmates were happy, too. I just went with the flow of the excitement. I told Tracey, who had been living as a live-in nanny, looking after a beautiful six-month old baby boy. She was working for two doctors who lived off the Las Vegas strip. She was so excited that I was getting married and was already planning what I should have at the wedding.

I was a marrying into a Mormon family: James was the total opposite to what my parents wanted – especially Dad. James was never going to be that, as I found out. He had other interests in mind. Dad always wanted me to marry a catholic Lebanese man who provided for the family and had a great job, like a doctor or lawyer.

Armed holdup

Coming Home: The Change in Me

'If you don't do anything today, your life tomorrow will be the same as it was yesterday.'

— Unknown

The day came when I boarded the plane bound for Australia. I said my goodbyes and off I went, back home to face my parents and find out what they thought of me getting married. Mind you, I never mentioned anything to them about me getting married; I thought I would wait until I faced them.

My heart skipped a beat when I saw the Sydney Harbour Bridge and the Opera House beneath me. I was happy to be home and to see my beautiful city again, but sad to see my dad especially. I was greeted by my parents at the airport and they asked me so many questions. My sister was excited to see me; she was nine years younger than me. All their questions were coming at me and all I could think of was how was I going to tell them that I was going to get married, just turning twenty-three and about to move to another country where I had no-one I really knew, and no family. This was going to take a big toll on my mother later down the track.

I spent the first few weeks catching-up with friends and going out to the local pubs and clubs. My time was spent at good old Studebaker, Traders, Argyle Street and PJ Gallagher's – all in Parramatta. We would venture out to the Castle Hill Tavern and Mean Fiddler. I was the type that liked to mix her outings and the people I mixed with. Now that I was back for a while, I wanted to hang out not just with my own culture and background but with different nationalities. So by going out in those three months, I managed to go out with a group of friends that were mixed: both in nationality and gender. I felt different, felt like an outsider: maybe because of my time aboard. I just felt that maybe I didn't fit in with my old group of friends from high school. I had experienced way too much in the year that I had travelled, while my friends were working and studying at university. I felt for the first time that my circle of friends was changing, not that I wanted it to, it just happened.

I finally managed to have a conversation with my parents about the whole getting married and living overseas things. My parents were so angry.

'We do not take divorce lightly and we will not have you shaming us again.'

'You know Dad, I'm sick and tired of you and Mum going on about your reputation and how it affects you both. I am not living by your rules or the way you think I should be going in my life. It's my journey and the mistakes I make are for me to learn from, not you.'

OMG – I just spoke back to Dad without screaming! I was calm, and I really did not care where my path took me. I was doing this on my own, which I believe made me realise I was becoming a young adult who had opinions and views and stood up to things that I thought were incorrect. I realised I had changed slowly, becoming just a bit wiser and stronger – becoming a person who was challenging my father and was not afraid of him, like I had been in the past.

I believe that we make choices in life and it's the choices you make that will create the path, whether it's a good choice or the wrong choice. It's up to us to learn from the path we choose. No-one is going to live your life but you, so go out and do something bold or risky – take that challenge: the one life you have is meant to be lived.

'Stop living for everyone else; live for you and you only.'

I took my own advice and I didn't give a damn about what my friends or what my parents' friends thought. My parents were always worried about what other people thought; that was their problem. Mum had spent her whole life looking after her three children, never being able to go out and enjoy being single for long enough. Dad was the only man in Mum's life; she married only to experience one man, and that is great in some people's eyes, but not in mine. I was going to learn this quite quickly in the years that followed. I have seen a lot of women get to an age and say 'what if', or they start rediscovering themselves at forty years old because they were young and got married and had their children and are now divorced. I cannot speak on behalf of all women: some women are happy and content with giving their whole life to their family, and I respect that, but for me I needed more. I was going to explore that.

Going back overseas was kept on the down low. Yes: my parents thought it was too shameful to speak to anyone about what I was doing, as in their circle of friends and mine, no-one just packed up and left to go abroad like that – let alone travel for almost a year. Regardless, I loved my parents, no matter what I went through with them – especially my dad. I understood that both my parents came out here to make a life for their family, and when that family started growing up in a country where the cultures were so different, it scared them. They wanted to raise us like they were brought up in Lebanon, and here I was: torn between the two cultures. I was first generation Lebanese–Australian and it was going to be a tough road to change and Westernise my father, though this would eventually happen after years of adapting to the way of life in Australia.

So for the next two months I made sure that I was out of Dad's way and also preparing myself for the trip back. I spent Christmas and New Year of 1995/96 in Sydney, and then come February 1996 I was going to the States. James always called me and spoke to me; to be honest I really did not know what love was. I thought I did, but thinking about it now, I was not in love. It was a ticket to get out of my situation and this was the only way I knew how.

My day came for me to say my goodbyes to Mum, my sister and my brother.

Dad said, 'I only have one daughter; you do not belong here anymore,' and turned away. My father had disowned me again; it was always such a roller-coaster ride with him. 'You are never to call this house again.' He turned his back from me and walked out of the room.

Mum cried. I just felt for her so much – I was causing her grief. I loved her, though my life needed to be lived. I felt that I was being held back been in Sydney and the environment I was in. I gathered my bags and off I went into the taxicab.

'Airport please driver.'

As tears streamed down my face, I looked back at the house I was raised in; would I ever see my family again?

My heart was beating as I took that step closer to the gate to board my plane to Los Angeles. I could turn back now, I thought. What was I getting myself into marrying someone I hardly knew? What life was I going to have with James? But this was the choice I had made.

I boarded, seating myself in business class. I owed it to myself to travel in style. I had accumulated enough points to travel business class one-way, and I needed it. I had a lot of thinking to do on this flight and I didn't want distractions.

'Have faith in yourself
Never give up
Try and Try again.'

The Wedding: Las Vegas Style

"Life is about taking risks. If you never take a risk, you will never achieve your dreams."

—Unknown

I spent a few months planning the wedding with my mother-in-law, as we had moved in with James' parents to save money. Here I was at twenty-three years old getting married. I was clueless – as was James, who was the same age as me. Though I just didn't see in him the ambition or drive to do something with his life. He was a runner: someone who worked for a law firm and ran mail jobs for them, sending important documents to clients. There was no way that I could see him doing this forever: he needed to do something more. We were about to get married – there had to be more drive than his pot-smoking and drinking and the job he was doing.

'James, what is it that you want out of life? You cannot be a runner; you need to look at the big picture. You're not a little boy anymore: you are getting married and we need to see that boat sail.'

He looked at me with those big brown eyes; I guess I made him think.

'I never really thought about it, Silvana.'

I could not turn back, I had a father who had disowned me, and I was going to prove him wrong – that I could survive without the family.

Well, the next day I was standing in the front yard of my in-laws' house playing with James' full-breed American pit bull, Sadie. She was dark brown with a white marking on her forehead, and she stood tall – right up to my hip. She scared even the toughest guy, though I grew very fond of her and she was beside me all the time so that she was practically mine. Then I saw a lady, Karla, running across the road to me. She stopped in her tracks, looking at Sadie.

'It's OK,' I said.

'Who are you?'

'I'm going to be James' wife soon and I'm here staying at my in-laws until the wedding.'

'Oh really? Is Meg here? I'm in trouble and I need her to babysit my little ones.'

'No-one is here except Sadie and me.'

She looked at me for a few seconds, then it was like a bright idea lit up in her mind and I could see the light switch on.

'You can babysit – please?'

'Me, babysit? I do not know how to look after a newborn or a three-year-old.'

'Yes, you can.'

So just like that I was babysitting; I put Sadie out the back, and she looked at me with those brown eyes that made me feel guilty.

'I'll be back Sadie!' I called out and watched her ears pop up in excitement.

Karla was so excited. Like most people in Las Vegas, she thought I was South African because of my accent – some mistook me for a New Zealander but hardly anyone thought I was Australian. She showed me the girls: Stacey, the newborn, was asleep and Jessica, the three-year-old, just looked at me. Karla explained that she had to go for a few hours and would be back soon, and explained to Jessica that I was looking after her. She gave me all the instructions and just like that she left.

I stood there staring at Jessica. What do I know about children? Especially looking after them. The only experience I had was maybe looking after my sister growing up. So I grabbed Jessica's hand and took her to the living room, where we played with her dolls. She was actually enjoying my company and vice versa. Then a cry came out from the bedroom, so I got up from the floor and walked with Jessica. Stacey was crying. I picked her up and held her in front of me, arms stretched in front.

'Oh boy, you smell.'

Jessica laughed at me. 'You need to change diapers,' this tiny voice muttered back.

I was in a state of panic and kept Stacey at arm's length. Well this was going to be a mission. I had never changed nappies before. So the challenge began, and here I was changing Stacey and pulling all these facial features that had Jessica in stitches.

'I'm glad, kid, that I can make you laugh.'

I managed to get through it, with a lot of sweat coming down from every part of my body. I finally had the two girls playing and laughing. I had no concept of time, until Karla walked in.

'Silvana you're a natural at this! I know you're not working at the moment, though you could start looking after the girls and be their part-time nanny. Gordon and I sometimes need to be out of town or going to events in the evening; the girls would love to have someone like you around.'

Gordon was a well-known real-estate lawyer in Las Vegas and was always out for meetings. Just like that, I accepted the offer. I made my way to my in-laws' house across the road and went out the back to tell Sadie the good news. After playing with Sadie, the family had come home from the day's work and I explained to James the job offer I got. He was happy, though surprised, that I had gotten such an offer.

So the wedding was a few weeks away, and Tracey had organised with Stephanie my girls night out. Both would be my bridesmaids, and Cathy (who I had met in Los Angeles) would be my other bridesmaid. Everything was paid for, but James' parents could not understand why no-one from my family wanted to come. I just didn't want to get into a conversation with them on such a heavy topic. His parents were amazing: organising every aspect of the wedding reception. I organised that we would get married in a beautiful Catholic chapel. The walls had hand paintings that were breathtaking. James and I had to go to classes before the big day to make sure that we were aware of the vows that we were about to take.

Stephanie, Tracey and I decided we would go and look for my wedding dress. I tried on the first dress in the first bridal shop on the strip – it was a halter neck and came out like a princess dress. Both the girls loved how it looked on me and that was that. I bought the first dress I tried on, a total of $500, and then got my shoes and accessories, and James' parents looked after the rest. I felt bad that they were paying for the wedding, and that my parents had no part of this due to Dad's stubbornness. I looked at the dress I had bought and felt loneliness come over me: did I have second thoughts about the wedding? I sure did. But I was going to make this work and prove to my father I could survive on my own, without having to be told how to live my life.

That evening, the girls organised a very wild hens' night. First, they picked me up from my in-laws' and put a blindfold on me. They left it on all the way to TGIF – a restaurant and bar that was a very happening place back then. I was instructed to lie down on the bar, and when I did, I felt someone licking my stomach. I jumped up and found a very handsome man standing in front of me downing a tequila shot. It was the bartender.

'What the hell is this?' I called out.

'It's your hen's night!' Everyone at the bar called out.

I laughed, as I got myself off the bar. The body shots continued for the rest of the hen's party. Though there were only four of us, I was happy with our intimate outing. We eventually ate there, as we had a long night ahead of us, and we didn't want to get drunk too early.

The blindfold had come on again and we were off to the second venue. I was led by someone's hand and, as we got there, I could hear a lot of people. Before you knew it, I was sitting on a chair. I was told to put my hand out and wait, and soon I felt skin on my hand and was told to take off the blindfold. There I was on stage with hundreds of screaming women and a cowboy stripper in front of me, with a six-pack to die for. I was in heaven. He put on a show for me, dancing almost on top of me in such a provocative manner. I had never been exposed like this before to a man who was so confident in his moves; this was all new to me.

After the show, the cowboy came up to me and he and his other workmate wanted to see if we would hang out with them – his mate had his eye on Stephanie. Stephanie was a glamourpuss: 5'9" with long dark hair, and she had Lebanese heritage from generations ago. She always turned heads with her looks. We declined the offer and made our way into the strip club. I wanted to see what it was like, never having been in one before. Though in Las Vegas, being in a strip club was not shameful: it was normal. A lot of people went in there to socialise before they went out.

Stephanie was just standing there looking glamorous and some guy came over and tipped her $50, just for looking beautiful. She got so excited and decided that she would buy us all a round of drinks. I was amazed that there were round dancefloors everywhere, with people watching these beautiful women perform – and not only were there woman dancing, on the other side of this massive club they also had male strippers. I was blown away to see all this: it was a mixed club catering to both genders.

The Wedding: Las Vegas Style

We left the strip club and I was blindfolded again. I ended up standing in front of somewhere with the music pumping loud. It was the popular club called the Beach House. We danced the night away, and I even got to go on the podium with my girls as the DJ knew it was a hen's night. I was so happy just dancing away until the sun came up.

James asked me how my night went. He was surprised that I did not have a hangover. I explained what we did and he was shocked that we had done all that in one night. He and his boys had ended up at a dive, according to James, and the night ended quite a bit earlier as everyone had passed out from being drunk. James was looking quite seedy himself.

The day arrived in May 1996. I made my way to the chapel that was off the Las Vegas strip. James' parents had invited 150 guests to the wedding and I only had three, who were my bridesmaids. James' father walked me down the aisle, which saddened me because I had a father who refused to attend the wedding. I held my tears back. I saw strangers around me, not my mother or my sister; I was so close to them and yet I felt so far away.

We exchanged our vows and made our way to the Desert Inn Sheraton Hotel, where we had photos taken on the golf course. I still have that wedding album and they were such beautiful photos. I am not ashamed of my past: it shaped me, and as you get older, you just gather more experiences. When we entered the reception lounge, I was blown away by the set up. The first thing I noticed was the two ice sculptures of swans with their heads touching together. So much went into this preparation and I went over to James' parents and thanked them for such an effort.

From there, a few of us went back to our hotel. Our honeymoon was three days staying in the three-bedroom penthouse suite at the MGM Grand. James' dad was the vice-president of the hotel and had organised the package for us. It was a breathtaking room, with sweeping views of the strip and the mountains. We arrived, to endless champagne being served.

James came up to me. 'You know, a lot of my parents' friends thought you had no family and that something tragic had happened.'

I looked at him and nodded my head, acknowledging his words.

'What did your parents say?'

'That they are back in Australia and could not make it to the wedding.'

So they still thought it was strange that no-one came over. I had my head down and then looked up at him. 'Ah well, call it an elopement on my behalf; my parents never approved and I went against their wishes.'

By now everyone was leaving, and James said he was going downstairs with his mates to celebrate a bit more.

Tracey and Stephanie thought it was strange that he was leaving me and offered to stay. I said it was fine and he should not be too long. I thanked them so much for their support and all their help. They made their way out and I was there, standing looking at the view. I walked over to the window and sat there looking at the strip below, watching the world pass beneath me. It was my wedding night and I had no husband to celebrate our commitment together.

Hours passed and I laid on the bed, looking at the ceiling with my wedding dress still on. I had tears coming down my face; I knew this marriage was not going to last and that I had made a mistake. But I was not a quitter and I was going to give this one hundred percent.

I woke up to James walking in the door. It was after 7am and he staggered in drunk. I was upset with him.

'How could you have done this, leaving me on our wedding night? Where were you all this time?'

'Downstairs. I lost track of time.'

This was not how it was supposed to be. He wanted to sleep with me and he was drunk. I had never been with another man and James was my first at twenty-two years old. When I first did it with him, it was awful – not the experience I had pictured. I never forgot it because it was painful and I hated it. This time was the same but with no pain: I was upset that I had to go through this. But to me, to be a good wife I would accept it and keep my emotions tight and never mention a word again about the night. I never said anything until months later when I met a woman that would change me in every sense.

James and I had booked a belated honeymoon trip to the Caribbean. In the meantime, I was adjusting to being a wife. I still had been looking after Jessica and Stacey, and helped their family move into a gorgeous mansion. I got my official permanent residency and now was out looking for work. My first real job was working in a jewellers and later on I ended up getting my first car on loan. I just didn't want to be a burden to anyone, and getting around on public transport back then was not the best. I remember visiting a friend who at the time had a neighbour who's friend was Andre Agassi, a famous tennis player, ranked as being an eight times' grand-slam champion. He was always driving around in his black Jeep Wrangler, with his long hair and different-coloured head bands. James and Jack (one of James' friends) would laugh at me because I didn't know who this great tennis player was. He would always greet us, as we were on the balcony above the entrance. Jack said one day that I should get a ride back with the ace player.

'No, I'll make my way home on my own.' As Jack didn't have a car, I did the next best thing: I hitched a ride. An old man picked me up.

'You are not from here, are you? Because people in Las Vegas – especially pretty ones like you – do not hitchhike. It's very dangerous and you are lucky I stopped rather than anyone else.' He gave me the biggest lecture, and he was right: I had put my life in danger.

He dropped me off at Stephanie's work, Caesars Palace. I thanked him so much and thought about what he had told me.

Stephanie worked selling high-end fashion and by now had broken up with our old flatmate Carlos. I waited around until she could drop me off. After this incident, I promised myself that I would not be a burden and so I took out a loan and bought a car.

James tried to teach me a few times in the Jeep, though I just could not drive a manual properly and really, what's the point of having a manual vehicle when there are so many stops and starts on the road? I told him that I was very happy driving an automatic, thanks.

'Judge me and I will prove you wrong. Say I'm not worth it, and watch where I end up.'

— Unknown

Masquerade

Life in Las Vegas: Discovering Myself

"There is no greater journey than the one that you must take to discover all of the mysteries that be within you."

—Michelle Sandlin

I was always out and about. James and I would explore Lee Canyon and go for hot chocolates up in the lodge, or I would try my hand at snowboarding, going to the pubs in the winter or out into the casinos. I always had a very tight friendship with Stephanie and by the summer, I was out partying and going to the clubs in town. Rio Hotel was a super club: I enjoyed just watching the women come in all dressed up. There was one that I will never forget, all dressed up in a white bikini and wearing a mesh dress; she did not leave much to the imagination. People danced in these clubs like no-one was watching.

I also explored canyons like Red Rock, with a waitress at our local pub and every weekend we hiked, before it got too hot. I would explore Laughlin and jet ski on the Colorado River with James. I would also hike by myself in the mountains, which my friends thought was crazy. Though I always registered my name with the ranger and told him which track I was going on.

One day I was hiking, and as soon I got to the top, this eagle circled me. I remember just watching it as it looked back at me. That moment felt spiritual. I had been struggling with James: he had no drive, and I would come home to find him drunk with his friends, lying on the ground passed out, or smoking pot. There were days that I would come home from work and see twenty-four beer bottles lined up on the coffee table. I was getting caught up in it myself, as I was in that environment every day; pot was so easy to come by and drinking and gambling was a problem for most people, as it was a twenty-four-hour city.

Sometimes I would drive while smoking pot at the same time and the lines on the road looked like they were one continuous line that was never ending. What was happening to me? This was not my life or the way I wanted to be. We would also argue a lot. I felt that

I was getting more depressed being with him and that his negative attitude just would not change. He was feeling sorry for himself and just didn't want to change.

I went to his parents, as I needed help with him. His friends were not a good influence and I encouraged James change jobs. His father organised work for him as a valet attendant. These were not easy jobs to get because the tips they got were enough to live off for the week. Working in the hospitality industry, you relied a lot on tips, as the wages were really low. I explained to James that I was off for the weekend to San Diego to visit a friend and her husband. I had met a girl called Koula, while they were here in Las Vegas, and she was a Greek–Australian who was born and raised in Perth. Her husband was a sergeant in the Marine Corp recruit depot. I needed some reassurances that James was going to change and better himself; I needed time out. I was working full-time at the jewellery store and looking after the two little girls when Karla had an event – which was every second night.

So I drove down to San Diego and was greeted by Koula and her husband; it was great to explore and even to be taken on the army base. It was funny, though, seeing the recruits: I felt I was getting fed to a pack of wolves, all sticking their heads out the window like they had never seen a woman before. Koula's husband, Brad, mentioned that I had nothing to worry about, and I enjoyed meeting some of the marines. My time there was short and sweet, though I had fun and invited Koula and Brad back to stay with us for New Year's Eve, as it was only a few months till then. It would be great for James to meet new people, instead of being in the same rut.

When I came back, I chatted to James about what he wanted. He said that he wanted to work on our relationship. I was all for giving it a go, but I did mention to him that I could not be responsible for everything: running the household and working two jobs. James was a shift worker, so a lot of the time I did not see him.

'Have you thought about going to college to do hospitality or management, like you wanted to?'

He said that he would enrol in community college, which he did.

We spent some more time doing some short breaks, like the Grand Canyon and the reservation of Native Americans, visiting all the paintings from hundreds of years ago on the walls of mountains. We even managed to go to Utah with James' brother and his girlfriend.

That was a magical time; her family had a cabin in the mountains and every morning we would wake up to deer feeding just metres away. This was a time I enjoyed and was grateful for every moment, what I had in the present moment and what I was experiencing.

When we got back, James was starting to hit the right path. He enrolled and started on the last semester and by now it was Christmas. Las Vegas experienced snow for the first time in twenty-five years – it was amazing. I stood outside and watched as each flake landed on me. I was like a little school kid, enjoying every moment to the point that I had my tongue out in the snow, experiencing the whole thing.

Koula and Brad spent New Year's Eve with us. My mother, who would talk to me behind Dad's back, sent me a stunning outfit that was gold with embroidered detail and was short, with a stunning top to go with it. It was so glamourous and fitted the Las Vegas scene. A moment came over me when I opened the package: my mother loved me and she showed it by sending me something that would show off my personality. This outfit made a statement and I looked amazing in it. I wore it proudly, as it had come from a place filled with love.

Stratosphere Tower is where we wined and dined. I was happy to be surrounded by people who back home I would have not come across. I looked down on the strip, with the city lights shining brightly. Midnight came and the fireworks went off from above the tower in front of us. The tower was the highest building back then, and it was an amazing experience as there was a roller-coaster above the tower that had people on it, for after the fireworks. I was happy: I was in my element. Slowly I was discovering Silvana.

It was a new year and I had big dreams and goals. The jewellery store I worked in was getting boring, but an Egyptian workmate that had moved to the Rio Hotel suggested that I apply to work with him in the watch store. As I had worked for five years in a jewellery store back home specialising in selling watches, I applied.

In the meantime, I had a two-week stint at the MGM Grand, thanks to my father-in-law. I was taking bookings for hotel rooms. It was awful; we were timed to see how long it took us to book a room, and we were timed to see how long it took us to go to the toilet. I could not be micromanaged. Just like that, I took the headphones off, got up and looked at the room that I was in. I went up to my manager and said that I could not do this anymore.

I left just like that, while everyone watched me. I never looked back; I needed something more in my life. I spoke to my father-in-law and thanked him. He suggested I become a cocktail waitress at MGM. Being a cocktail waitress at the major hotels was not a job that could come easy and I could not see myself in a provocative outfit, walking around in heels for hours on end with men asking for my number and trying to chat me up. I thanked him but said that I needed to do something for me without relying on someone else to get me a job. I hope he understood.

I think James' dad had a different view of me now that he knew I was not after money or a ticket to get me into a job. He realised that I wanted to do things on my own – be my own person. Many people these days rely on networking and on other people to get them work. He mentioned that being a vice-president of a major hotel he would get a lot of random people asking for favours. I was not inclined to be like that.

I got the job at Rio Hotel and worked different hours, due to late trading. I loved it: it was the only place that had a carnival that went around the hotel. I was invited a few times to join the dancers – to get dressed up in the masquerade and throw beads down to the people on the casino floor and play the tambourine.

My life was changing because I was allowing the good energy to come through. After work, I would meet Stephanie at the bar next door. We became friends with the bar staff, who made us laugh, and we enjoyed the atmosphere.

My relationship with my workmates was amazing. I was close to an Egyptian male and a Spanish woman, both much older than me – maybe in their early forties – and they always looked out for me.

By now, life was streaming along fine. My uncle came over from Paris and spent some time with me in Las Vegas. Tracey had adjusted to life back home. I was still in contact with Abbey and her husband Brendan, the two doctors, and I would occasionally look after their little boy. I also would still look after Karla's children. So life was getting busy and I was becoming more independent, while James was working different shifts to me and studying.

Spring was here and I used to always hang out with Gordon, a mate that I worked with at the jewellers. He was a sales representative for Budweiser now, and Stephanie and I would always go to the pool parties they would hold. James would come when he was free, though was never happy; it was like I had to always make sure that he was comfortable. I felt like he was dragging me down, as I was a free spirit who enjoyed life and what it had to offer. Everything with him was doom and gloom. I was changing – growing in a direction that James didn't want. He didn't want to change at all: he was back to smoking pot and drinking. Don't get me wrong, I drank and smoked a bit of pot here and there too, but not doing it every day like I used to.

I decided that I was going to live and try and be as happy and positive, regarding the situation I was in, so I joined a twenty-four-hour gym. I wanted to work on myself and be happier and healthier. It was all so new to me: you had very fit people in the gym and I was trying to figure out the weights and equipment. I tried a few times, then I noticed a class that had about forty people in it. I walked over and watched as two instructors were showing boxing moves and kicks. This was more like me. I came back and joined the combat class and I loved it. I found my love for fitness.

James was not too happy that I was training at a gym, and I felt that I was out-growing him. I tried to talk and to help – even when I came home and the place was a mess I would just clean, without saying a word to him. But I would only put up with so much before the bubble would burst. I was enjoying my independence and was finally enjoying my own company and discovering myself. This was something I had not had at home because I was overshadowed by Dad and sheltered from the real world.

I looked forward to being at the Rio Hotel more than being in my relationship, which I thought was holding me back. By now, Santos and Tomas, the bartenders that worked next door to the watch store, had moved to the main bar downstairs, which was better for them. I would go there after work and wait for Stephanie to come; I was always looked after with cocktails. The boys put on a show mixing them and always drew a crowd to the bar – watching the movie *Cocktails* with Tom Cruise was nothing like what these guys could do.

A few times I was approached by men drinking on their own. One time, a guy left a spare card and mentioned his room number.

'Sorry I am married, not interested.'

'Well if you change your mind, this is my room number and I'll look after you money-wise.'

Now, Santos and Tomas had seen this on a few occasions while I was waiting for Stephanie. And even when Stephanie was there, men would come up to us offering money.

'Guys what is going on? This is all new to me,' I had said, and they laughed, knowing that I was clueless.

'Silvana, you are handling yourself fine. We would have stepped in if there was a problem.'

'Those men think you're an escort.'

'What? I'm not even dressed like one.'

'High-class escort,' Tomas said, 'You're here almost every second day and they think you're working. They don't know you work in a watch shop. Besides, you are exotic looking in their eyes. These guys have plenty of money and just want a beautiful woman like yourself and Stephanie around them. It is normal in Las Vegas, don't be offended: take it as a compliment. Never judge women who do that line of job, they are educated women and some are supporting a family. Some even have homes paid off and are putting their children through private schools.'

'How do you know all this, Tomas?'

'They come here and talk to us; some have been here while you have been at the bar. Never judge anyone, Silvana. These ladies can get $5000 a night.'

'I understand,' and I looked sheepishly at Tomas.

So I walked away and thought hard. Tomas was right: never judge people, no matter what walk of life they have come from. Being around family and friends back home, people were so easy to judge and yet again I felt grateful that I was exposed to people who I would not have met back home. I learnt to accept people that day. If they are good to you, no matter what their background, be polite and never judge.

The Turning Point

'Surround yourself with people who push you,
Who challenge you,
Who make you laugh,
Who make you better,
Who make you happy.'

— Ali Krieger

After a few months passed I needed a change: I was getting tired working in a casino. Stephanie introduced me to a lovely husband-and-wife team: Dianne and Semon. He was from Israel and had married an American beauty, who back in the seventies was one of the first waitress bunnies for the famous Studio 54 nightclub. She had lived as an actress in New York. Dianne and Semon moved to Las Vegas where they opened their store, Stash Clothing, and along the way had four children.

Dianne was looking for someone to help in their high-end, funky, mix-gendered labels. Most people who knew their labels knew of this store. The collection they carried was different and did not follow the normal retail stores. If you wanted something different, you came here. I was hired, even though I didn't know fashion, but I was keen to learn about each label they carried.

Dianne showed me the true way to sell and up-sell. Customer service was very important, and you had to treat everyone like they were special. I learnt very quickly that there were some famous and rich customers, along with the socialites that frequented the store every week for something new.

This one particular day, I was gathering the garbage in the morning and was heading out. An African–American man walked into the store. I had seen him pull up in a black SUV with an entourage of six black Dutch bikies. I ran straight into his hard stomach. I apologised, not knowing who the hell he was and he smiled at me, knowing I was clueless. Semon waited until I came back, then went out with the guy named Mike Tyson, who had given me a credit card.

'Can you please put three outfits together for my girl? I trust your taste, and money is no problem.'

'OK,' I said, 'I will wrap them up for you also, as it sounds like it's a gift. Your woman is lucky to have you around.'

'I love your accent,' Mike Tyson said, still smiling and nodding his head; clearly I didn't know who he was.

Sisa, who was another employee at the time, turned to me and mentioned that Semon had cancer and that he was going through chemotherapy.

'Mike Tyson – that guy that spoke to you – is the boxing heavyweight champion of the world. He's at his prime – everybody knows who he is.'

'Well Sisa, I do not follow boxing: how should I know who he is?'

'Boxing is a big thing in Vegas and he's going to be fighting in a few months to hold his title,' she told me.

Semon and Mike Tyson came back from their boost drinks – which I'd never heard of before, though it was such a craze for everyone to drink healthy smoothies. I gave Mike Tyson his clothing and his credit card and he was off, entourage and all.

I saw Semon in a different way after that; he had four children and a business and was going through cancer ... I had such respect for him and his wife. These people would not only help me through a tough situation soon, they would help rebuild me in a way that would shape me to become the independent lady that I am today. I worked hard over the next month, bringing in the money for Stash Clothing. I loved selling clothes and meeting different people.

Mike Tyson was fighting in September 1996 at the MGM Grand against Bruce Seldon. I was undergoing a change: I wanted to box and become not just physically stronger, but more mentally focused. I thanked Mike Tyson, as I watched him fight on occasions, though he did not know the effect he had on me. It was watching him fight and having him come in every week to Stash Clothing, when he would take Semon out for their chats that got me into boxing. Boxing really helped shape me to become sharp, both physically and mentally. Even though it's a tough and lonely sport, I was going to beat the odds and I was going to make a mark as a female boxing

The Turning Point

coach. When a sport is dominated by males, it is a cutthroat world for a woman to enter the industry.

> 'I do it for the passion, the hunger; I do it to claim my mark in a small way.
> Fear the ones that are observant and walk silent, in this world. They are the ones that are accomplished in life.'
>
> — Unknown

Mike Tyson won the World Boxing Heavyweight Championship title via a technical knockout (TKO) in the first round. That night made a mark on the rap music world also; a world famous rapper, Tupac, was shot outside the MGM Grand and died a few days later. It was the most talked-about night. I was at the MGM Grand, though left an hour beforehand. passing his famous nightclub, which was only a few blocks from where I lived, called 666; it always had people waiting for hours to get inside.

There it was, just like that: life can be taken away, no matter who you are.

Airforce base

Dianne and Semon, Stash Clothing

Cancer Hits, Making Me Stronger

'Success isn't just about
What you accomplish in your life,
It's about what you inspire.'

— Unknown

I had been sitting on a chest-press machine at the gym and noticed a lump in my right middle finger, down on the palm of my hand. It played on my mind for some time.

It was coming close to the end of the year and I had great news that my friend from high school would be staying with me over the New Year. Even though things with James were a bit shaky now, I still went on with my day-to-day business.

Dianne and Semon had bigger issues: they were heading towards bankruptcy. They believed in their dreams for the shop so much and were fighting to keep the dream alive. The medical bills had taken a toll on the family, with looking after Semon's treatment. I so wanted to help in any way that I could, but I was about to face my own challenges.

End of 1997, I was sitting at a doctor's office – mind you, this doctor was not much older than me – as my lump had gotten so big that I could not close my hand properly anymore. It was a size of large grape.

'Silvana, we need to take a biopsy of the lump. This is very strange that you have something like that on your hand. Let's not come to any conclusions until the test results come back.'

I had told James about this, but he was not too worried. By this time, he had quit his job as a valet parker and also quit his studies because he failed a few subjects and didn't want to go back and finish. Now more than ever I was dealing with looking after the household. He was off work for three months. I knew I had made a mistake with this relationship, though my father had always told me that once you got married, you stayed in the relationship; there was no such thing as divorce.

A week later, the doctor gave me news.

'Silvana, you have a tumour that is growing on your right hand. I have never come across anything like this before as a doctor: it's grown fast and we need to operate on this next week. It's aggressive, and you are lucky that it's in the finger because it will not spread quickly through the body – it will stay centralised in the hand. If anything, you will probably lose your middle finger, as it's sitting on the nerves, and you will also lose feelings in some of your fingers.'

I looked at him in silence. How was I going to handle this challenge?

'Silvana, are you OK? Is there someone I can call, or get someone to chat with you?'

'No. All good.'

Here I was at twenty-five years old on my own, with no family, dealing with another health issue. My mother was not around, and my husband was not the support I wanted around me.

I contacted the two doctors, Abbey and Brendon, because I looked after their little boy from time to time. Abbey decided that she would do her part for free and wanted to make sure that there was someone there for me, as I had no family around me. She was an atheist and Abbey felt for me and thought it was her duty to make sure I was looked after.

'Silvana, you are very strong. This is not an easy operation, and it will take about two hours.'

The universe was looking after me; I had an angel in the name of Abbey. I knew I was going to be fine – I had to believe this was going to be fine.

The day arrived, and I was admitted. James had taken me to the hospital, and the operation went well. I was grateful, because when I opened my eyes, Abbey was there holding my hand.

'They saved your finger, and you will gain some feelings in your fingers in months to come. Silvana, you are so lucky – that was a nasty tumour, and it could have spread to your body. You trusted your gut and went to see the doctor about the lump.'

The doctor showed me the tumour: it was bigger than I thought. I was lucky to have that removed.

Now it was time for rehab, to get my hand back to full working potential. The doctors feared that I would lose thirty percent of movement, but I was not going to take no for an answer; I was going to work at it.

The following week, my friend came and stayed with us in our one-bedroom apartment. I had told her that I had surgery, but she wanted to stay with us. It was such bad timing, though I did my duty as best as I could to accommodate her. I even went out on the Las Vegas strip with them, though I asked James to start showing them around as I just could not do it. I didn't have the physical strength. my two friends stayed with us for four days then were off to finish their trip. I mentioned to Dianne that I would be back at work the following week, if everything went well. They had managed to save the shop and they also decided that they would move to a new part of Las Vegas and also move the shop to Summerlin. I was happy to be a part of the move.

While I was still recovering, there was one night that James and I had an argument about him working. Things got heated and I just could not cope with handling all the financial matters; I needed him to pull his weight. I was against the wall in the tiny dining room and James picked up a chair and threw it at me. I moved, but it hit the hand I'd had surgery on. I was in shock and in pain; I was not going to have another male lay a hand on me. James collapsed on the floor in a foetal position and was rocking back and forth.

'James, are you OK?' I was more worried about him than me. 'I'm calling 911, you are freaking me out.'

He mentioned that he had been taking something to feel better. I asked him what medication he was taking, and he said that they were prescription pills.

I called 911 and the operator knew straight away that there was domestic violence. She told me everything I said was a yes or no answer over the phone. She could tell from my voice that there was a situation. I asked for an ambulance for James, and within ten minutes of hanging up the phone, there was a knock on the door. I answered the door to find two massively built police officers. They came in and asked about my hand, and whether it had happened tonight.

'No,' I answered, 'I have just come out of surgery for having a tumour removed. I'm still not one-hundred percent.'

One police officer asked what happened, while the other questioned James. The police officer came back scratching his head.

'Your husband has just mentioned that you tried to kill him with a knife.'

I could not believe what was coming out of James' mouth.

'Well, officers, you can see the broken chair on the ground and you can see my right hand has been operated on. I'm right-handed,' I was staying calm. My hand was bleeding from protecting myself from being hit in the face from the chair. I could not believe what was happening.

The officers could see what was going on and asked if I had anywhere to go to stay the night. I said I had no family and had only been in the States for close to two years. They stayed until James got his parents to pick him up. The officers laid no charges on James, as I said there was no need – even after he accused me of trying to kill him. The officers and I could see he was heavily medicated. He did not want to go to hospital.

His parents arrived, and James said yet again that I had tried to harm him. The officers explained to James' parents, and then waited until James and his parents had left the premises before leaving. They said that I had held it together pretty well considering I had just come out of hospital, and if I needed anything to contact them.

I closed the door and walked to the balcony. It was such a beautiful night. I looked up to the brightest star and thanked the universe and God for looking after me and keeping me safe. I also decide it was time for me to move out and leave James. I felt numb, having no-one to talk to, and feeling saddened by the whole experience.

The next day, I called James' parents and mentioned that I was moving out that day and that I would only take my car and the clothes – the rest was for James. I said that he could keep the honeymoon that we had planned together in the Bahamas.

I spoke to Dianne about what had happened. Without thinking, she took me into their new home. She told me that I was such a trustworthy employee, that I could stay with them rent-free. I could not believe what I was hearing. The following week, I was back at work, helping them – using my good arm move into the Summerlin store.

I spoke to my mother about what had happened. She cried. She could not believe what had happened with my tumour and having surgery and what James had done. She begged me to come home.

'Mother, I need to do this for me and be away from the family. I have to work my life out on my own. Please understand.'

My father still was not on talking terms with me, which was OK; I was going to figure this out on my own, mistakes and all, and learn from that. My mother wanted to speak to Dianne about what had happened. Dianne promised my mother she would look after me like her own daughter, and she did, until the day I left the States.

'Be the kind of woman that makes other women want to be you.'

A road less travelled

Door Opens to New Opportunities

'Open the door. It may lead you someplace you never expected.'

— Unknown

I was working hard three times a week getting my hand back to normal with physio. The physio made me carry a tennis ball everywhere to work on the strength in my right hand. I had stopped going to the gym, as I was now living on the other side of town.

Life had changed for me. James was working hard to try to win me back, but I needed time as what he did was not right – whether or not he was medicated heavily and in a dark time in his life. It's usually the ones that are close to you that you hurt most, and time and time again in my life I've been hurt by the people that are close to me. I needed to live, and Dianne was there to help me discover the new woman in me. She mentioned it was time for me date other men.

'It's too soon, to date other men.'

'No, it's not; not after what you have been through. It's time to meet new people – look at you! You can have anyone.'

I could not believe what I had been through, first with my father, then my health, then James, but Dianne ignited the fire in me. I needed to be happy and explore life. If people hurt you, it's really about them – their insecurities – and I was learning that I should not let that affect me (easier said than done!).

Things did change: I met Emily from next door, who worked in a homewares shop. We hit it off from the word go. She had a young daughter and had a husband who was so understanding. He got the picture of her having her independence, which made it easier when we went out everywhere together and explored Las Vegas – especially the night life.

One day, an African–American man walked in and heard me serving a customer. I always looked out to see who was in the store.

He was over six feet tall and very distinguished. After I finished closing the sale, he approached me. He introduced himself as Rod. He gave me his card. I looked at it, he was a producer for a radio station called KLAV 1230 AM. He mentioned that he liked my voice and asked if I would like to set up a time with him to audition to be a co-host alongside him every Sunday.

'Rod, I have no experiences in radio. Why me?'

As I looked at him, this had to be a joke or a prank for MTV. I was looking to see if he had a hidden camera on him, or if there was anyone outside filming the whole thing.

'Is this a prank show?' I asked.

'No, it's not: I would really like you to come to the studio. You can even bring someone if you want, if you do not feel comfortable.'

Rod excused himself and left. I mentioned it to Dianne and Emily that day and they said I was to go for it.

So that week I went in, and even though I was feeling nervous, I made it through; he loved my voice and style. I was offered a regular gig every Sunday as a co-host, introducing up-and-coming new bands on the airways of Las Vegas. It was all voluntary work, though one door closed and another opened.

Things happened quickly. I meet another female who was hosting another segment after our show: Madison. We became very close friends and would give each other tips for being on live radio.

The new store at Summerlin was taking off; I was getting the rich, the socialites and the dancers coming in. I was getting invites everywhere and, I admit, I was feeling a bit insecure and refusing. Dianne said that I was no different to anyone else, money or not. I just felt that these clients were way out of my league. She helped me understand and taught me that no-one who walked in the door was better than me; we were all on the same playing field.

'Clients want to hang with you 'cause of your energy and your positive attitude. You have the package – you just do not realise your inner and outer beauty. It's time you started hanging out with people, regardless of status, and mixing up your social circle. Networking is good, especially if you are doing radio. You need the confidence.'

I took everything on board and made friends quite easily. I felt I had been restricted with James when I was with him, and felt he was holding me back because of his negative attitude. Sometimes in life, you get people that will weigh you down, and either you speak up or you're going to have to choose whether to cut your ties. Here I was, a free spirit and enjoying my new-found self. I felt like a weight was lifted off my shoulders and I was beginning to spread my wings in every sense.

I was invited to a dance cabaret at the Bailey's Hotel on the strip. Hannah, who came into the shop every week and bought clothes from a variety of labels, Ms Sixty to the French label Morgan, invited me – though her invite was like no other. I was to meet her backstage midweek, as she performed there four nights a week.

Backstage, I was surrounded by frantic, topless women running around getting ready. There were also men who were in the show performing. Hannah was excited I was there and had me watching from the dressing room; you could actually see the show from there. What a view. I was served food and champagne and could not believe I was sitting there.

'You are surrounded by real showgirls and guys,' a voice came from behind. I turned around to see a shirtless man standing in front me. I blushed; he had the perfect shape, six-pack and all.

'Darren's the name; I'll be jumping on soon with your friend Hannah.' He oozed confidence, with his piercing blue eyes and blonde hair that was bleached from the Las Vegas sun. 'You're lucky to be here, backstage and watching the show. Enjoy the experience. I got to go: I'll see you around soon.'

Just like that he disappeared, and I could see him dancing in the show. Wow. I was so grateful just sitting here watching the true showgirls and guys dancing from their hearts; their passion and grace ignited the room, with their smiles and graceful moves.

The show finished and Hannah came up to me.

'What did you think of the show?'

'I thought you were amazing Hannah! You're perfect.'

'Well you can come on Saturday and watch me perform at the Hard Rock Hotel.'

That was the same place I had met James: back then it was the place where everyone wanted to be seen. I agreed to go.

Dianne asked how I went at the show.

'I loved it! She asked me to go see her perform at the Hard Rock on Saturday, but I have no-one to go with.'

'You do not need anyone to go with – you will be surprised what happens when you're on your own. Look at it as an adventure.'

Saturday night came and I was told to go on to the dance floor. So I danced by myself, and before you knew it Hannah came to the middle of the podium, dancing a storm. Her body was rocking. She moved in a way that before long I had guys come up to me and give me their numbers for Hannah to have. I smiled, Hannah kept looking at me smiling and laughing: she was in her element, and I was happy just watching her dance. Her infectious attitude had come over me and I danced, not knowing I was being watched by a client of Stash Clothing.

A few days later, Dianne came up to me and mentioned that I had some explaining to do. I was beside myself. On my day off, a gentleman left two tickets for me to accompany him to watch The Temptations, as he had enjoyed watching me dance and have fun on my own at the club.

'See what happens when you are carefree and happy? You must have really impressed him.'

She mentioned that the gentleman who left the tickets was very wealthy. He had given me a date and time for our special date.

So the day came, and at 5 pm I was ready. Dianne had made sure my make-up and hair were done and the black dress I wore was a number: slim-fitted with a spilt that ran up to my thigh and a collar that opened up just enough to show my cleavage.

Dianne and the kids danced around me and even Semon had a smile on his face. This was my second family: they were really happy that I was happy. Emily waited outside as a black limo pulled up and the driver came around and opened the door. I stepped into the vehicle, and there he was in a black suit.

Ashton looked amazing; he was a guy that came into the store every week to buy something. He always wore black Armani, and his aftershave would have wooed any woman. I sat beside him; he was smiling from ear to ear. I waved to my family and Emily as the limo drove off.

'I have organised our first stop for dinner at the Rio Hotel, five-star dining.'

That was where I use to work! I looked at him and my eyes widened with excitement. I might see my friends Tomas and Santos.

We pulled up to the front doors where the driver opened the

door and we stepped out. I walked through, past the bar where I used to sit when I had finished working at the watch shop, and the boys didn't recognise me at first – they had to look twice. They were all smiling.

'Enjoy your night Silvana,' they all spoke at once. Santos and Tomas were just nodding their heads and smiling.

We sat down to a wonderful dinner. Ashton made sure that everything was Australian, as he knew I was missing home and wanted everything presented on the table to be at its finest. As a customer at Stash Clothing, I had served him a few times and he had gathered by my accent that I was Australian. He knew I was home sick because he had asked Dianne about what I liked and didn't like.

He explained his reason for taking me out: that he was happy to see someone who didn't judge him for what he had – I treated him like anyone who walked into the store. He talked about when he saw me out dancing by myself.

'You didn't care who was watching. You are a confident woman, and I loved seeing a woman with a character like that.'

Ashton explained about his life, how he got married to an older woman and had two children. His wife was there for him when he had a brain tumour – you could see the scar that went along the right side of his hair line to his ear. I didn't ask about it; I believe that if someone wants to volunteer information, they will. I hate asking about someone's private life, unless they are willing to share. I have always been one to give advice and then listen if the person wants to talk.

He was not in love with her anymore and told me that he built an empire and was not enjoying his life; his children meant so much to him, and that watching me on Saturday night was a reminder that he needed to enjoy his life a bit more. We raised our glasses for that and continued the night. We went to the Desert Inn to watch The Temptations perform; we had a booth right at the front. To watch them sing 'My Girl' was amazing. Ashton even got up and sang with them – it was great to watch him let go and be in the present moment. From there, we went to a club and danced away the night.

Ashton invited me back to his hotel room. He took my hand and led me to the bed where we both laid and chatted more. He gave me a rose, and we kept chatting until he fell asleep. I left the rose beside him, then got up and lent over to kiss his forehead. I made my way to the door, and as I opened it, I looked back. I knew he had to figure things out and he was at a crossroads. Besides, I was going through my own thing, which I hadn't told him. He was a great guy, though we had met at the wrong time, and I was willing to let that go – even though he wanted more from me, I could not give it to him. Although things would have been very comfortable with him and I would have had no worries, I do not think I would have been happy with him. I had my journey, and it was not with him in my life.

Everyone asked how it went with Ashton;

'It was great, though I am not ready for someone who is going through his own complications; I do not want to be the rebound woman. I am happy to hang with him and be friends, though that is all I can give him.' Everyone respected my decision. Emily and Stephanie mentioned most women would have jumped to be with a millionaire, instead I just let it go.

'You are a very strong woman, Silvana.'

I knew that I did not need a man to make me feel accomplished; you need to be happy and confident within yourself – having a person like Ashton is a bonus, and it was not my time to have someone like that in my life. I was trying to discover myself.

The following week, it was my birthday, and the lioness wanted to play. So Stephanie and Emily came with me to two gigs that I had to MC for. The first one was at a private home, a mansion set in the valley of Summerlin, and the second one was introducing an up-and-coming Los Angeles band at a happening bar on the strip. I introduced the band in front of hundreds of eager fans, and I had just come off stage to wait for my friends to come back from the bar when a gentleman came up to me and started a conversation. He wanted me to join him, as he was new to Las Vegas and wanted to hang out with someone. By that time, the girls had come over and I needed to go to the toilet. When I came back, Stephanie (the sneaky girl) had told the guy, Dean, that it was my birthday.

We decided to move to another venue, and as I was organising to hail a cab, a limo pulled out in front of us. The driver got out and opened the door.

'Here you go, birthday girl.'

I looked back at the girls. 'Funny,' I said, 'who organised this?'

'I did,' Dean smiled. 'I want you to come with me and enjoy the night.'

'No; with all due respect, I came out with my girlfriends, and if they cannot come with us, then it's a no.'

So the decision was made and Dean had all of us in the limo. It was such an amazing night. Girls want to have fun, and fun they got! We drank, bar hopped, and I got to do the one thing I wanted: put my head out of the limo's sunroof as we drove down the Las Vegas strip.

Then I took it one step further and put my legs out. I was hanging upside down, and we dared each other to take our bras off and hang out the limo windows. Dean and the driver were in stitches. We ended up asking the driver to take us to a mountain that was just outside Las Vegas. We all sat on the roof of the limo and raised our glasses to living life, as you have only got one. We stayed there and watched the sunrise it was the start of a new day.

A few weeks later, I was asked to go to dinner with some influential women, some of whom had their own businesses and others that had husbands in politics and were quite well-known in Las Vegas.

'Dianne, why are they asking me out? I have no money – I'm just a woman working in retail and radio.'

I decided that in that year I would put myself through community college and get more education and qualification in radio and been a on air presenter.

'Have you thought that maybe it's the way you treat them? You treat them on the same level when they come into the store. You are honest and you're straight to the point. People like that: it's rare to find good, loyal people.'

I thought about it. I *was* good: I had a good character and I was able to pick up on the toxic people around me.

By now, I had finished going to college for broadcasting radio classes. I was also doing voiceovers and commercials on radio for KLAV 1230 AM. I was still making amends with James; his father had been promoted and now worked as the President of the New Hotel, New York, New York. It was the time when Lady Diana had died, and people were also talking about the Mike Tyson fight two months ago at the MGM because he had bitten off Evander Holyfield's ear.

I spent the night before the dinner picking the label off my shiny black pants. I knew these women wore nothing but labels, and I wanted to look right for the next day.

The dinner night came and I made my way to Caesars Palace to

Spago, a restaurant where the rich and famous dine out. I got there and found Cleo, my client from the shop. I was nervous and excited at the same time. We made our way to the table that was reserved for us. Fifteen women from different backgrounds showed up. We had even paparazzi and people who were dining asking for autographs from some of the woman on the table. I didn't want to ask who some of these women were.

The night went very well, and all I could hear were the women talking about travelling to New York over the weekend for shopping, and others going on a safari to Africa in two weeks and how some of their husbands were away on business trips.

Then the attention drew to me. I explained what I did, how I got to Las Vegas and what I was doing. I was waiting for their noses to turn up, as I was nothing like them and didn't live in their world. Instead, I got told I was a brave, strong woman. They even said they wished they were more like me: very independent. Some even said they couldn't do anything without asking their assistant or husband. I didn't feel so bad after that. Why did I feel uncomfortable in my own skin when there were people looking at you from different coloured lenses? I learnt a lesson, that we are no different from anyone else. No matter what we do in life, at the end of the day we all die and we take nothing with us. I was never going to be ashamed ever again, about where I had come from. My background was not going to own me.

The ladies all decided to make a trip to the Gucci store in Caesar's Palace and it was incredible watching the Japanese tourists asking for photos of some of these ladies. I still could not grasp who I was associating myself with, and still to this day I do not know. Some things, I guess, are best left a mystery.

A few weeks later, I was working in the store when my friends Darren and Hannah (the showgirl and guy) came in. They always made an entry by dancing and it made everyone in the store just that much happier. I had a stream of different social groups in my life. As Darren and Hannah continued shopping for their next weekend outfit, a group of guys walked into the store, had a look around, and walked out. Then one of the guys came back and asked me if he could have my number. At first I was not sure, and then I was like, what the hell! So I gave it to him and Hannah and Darren smiled from ear to ear.

'You go girlfriend! That was a very cute guy.' They both looked at each other nodding their heads.

Door Opens to New Opportunities 79

Emily came in, 'Did you see that group of guys that walked past? They must have come in the store.'

'Sure did, one of them actually asked for my number,' I looked at the ground, being all shy.

'You go girl!'

Within an hour, I got a phone call to the store. Matt was the name of the gentleman who had asked for my number. He wanted me to meet him after work for a coffee. I did, and we chatted for hours. We ended the night with him asking me if I was working in the morning and to keep an eye out for a flying bird at a certain time. 'Sure,' I said, thinking it's probably Big Bird from *Sesame Street*.

The morning came, and soon enough I heard a loud noise. Emily and I walked outside the store and before long, a military Blackhawk flew past, with Matt there on the doorway, waving. I waved back at him, shaking my head: very impressive. Now this was a way to win a woman's heart.

Matt, you sneaky person – you're in the air force! He must have been stationed at Nellis Air Force Base in Las Vegas. I got a call from him a few hours later.

'Well, Matt, nice way to tell me that you are in the air force.'

He did not want to be cocky and he thought it was the best way to show what he did for work. I never knew exactly what he did, as it was all classified and I respected his wish, but he did mention that he always had to parachute for training. I was to meet him again after work and wait for him outside the store.

Yet again, he surprised me, with six Hummers pulling up outside the store, women and men in the Jeeps; the surprise was that Matt wanted to take me to the desert at night. That is where they all gathered for a drink and bonfires and just chilled. I was given night-vision googles and was told to look outside. The sky was a different world. I could see the stars and satellites moving past us, it was breathtaking. I also got a chance to drive through the desert, though he said I was to drive with no lights and use my night-vision googles to get me through to where everyone was meeting. He trusted me, and like that, I did it – what an experience. He helped me enjoy the unknown and to have no fear. I learnt something that I didn't think I could do. It was a great night and I enjoyed everybody's company.

Matt was different: he showed me life in a different way. I began to appreciate life around me and what we had more and more. There were a few times he took me on base, and his squadron were all so pleasant. We began hanging out more and more. I realised that James did not show me the respect that I needed as a wife, friend and lover, though I was still debating about going back to him because of my father's words about not getting a divorce.

I would bring Matt into my world. I always took him out dancing to the great clubs in Vegas. Emily and Matt's friend Stewart would always hang out with us; it was great just to let your hair down. I could see in Matt's eyes there were times he wanted to escape. I knew with the job he had, it was not something you could just sit and talk about with anyone. I guess he respected that I knew what was going through his mind. I never questioned what he saw, or what he did for work. I was happy to have met him and enjoyed his friendship while I had it.

The next week he was on a mission for a month or more. He could not tell me where he was going, but it was a time of great unrest in the Middle East and the Gulf …

'At every moment
We need cheerfulness
To surmount all our problems.'

—Sri Chinmoy

The Terrifying Accident: Going Home

'For to be free is not merely to cast off one's chains, but to live in a way that respects and enhances the freedom of others.'

—Nelson Mandela

Matt had taken off to (supposedly) the Gulf, and for a while I was experiencing name calling and being called a Saddam Hussein relative. Saddam Hussein was the leader of Iraq, and was widely condemned for the brutality of his dictatorship. The total number of Iraqis killed by his security services in various purges and genocides was in the hundreds and thousands. The United States had stepped in after he invaded Kuwait and invaded Iraq to bring him down. Due to my surname being very similar to his, it got to the point that I was told to go back to where I came from.

I was not going to allow my surname and my background to change me.

I asked Santos, who was working at the bar at the Rio Hotel, if he could come with me to get a tattoo of my name in Arabic. As he had so many on him, he ended up taking me to a lady off the strip who could do what I asked for. It's funny, how the universe works; I asked my mother if she could fax me the word, as we did not have emails and internet access then like we do now. She refused to do it and did not believe getting a tattoo was a nice thing for a lady to do.

One day, a Lebanese lady walked into the shop with her daughter – and this was very rare, as there were hardly any Lebanese that I had heard of living in Vegas. She walked in, and I explained to her what I needed and the reason why. Without any hesitation, she wrote it down on a piece of paper, and there I had my name in Arabic. It was meant to be. I trusted that what she wrote was correct because I showed her a photo of my mother and told her how important it was for me to do this. This woman had walked in the shop and I would never see her come in again: it was a sign.

If I say I'm going to do something, I am going to do it. My mother knew how determined I was when I had something in my mind that I was going to do. I went with Santos, and I did not back down: the name in Arabic was put on my left ankle. I also got my star sign, Leo, in ancient hieroglyphs. It's there to remind me to never to be ashamed of my heritage due to what a minority have done.

Matt had a few missions, though I kept seeing him and kept being in awe of his presence. He had such an effect on me that I wanted to be a better person, because he was a good person.

One night, we had all gone to Matt's place. I was dared to drink Tequila shots with another guy; bets were placed. They lined up fourteen shots each: it was game on. All the boys thought that this was going to be an easy win for my contender because he was male. So guess who all the bets were going to? Not me, that was for sure.

I remained cool, just standing there and waiting and watching like a lion who was about to go for the kill.

We got the go.

I managed to finish off before the contender and won. He stopped at ten shots. The whole room went silent.

'Never judge a book by its cover!' I called out as I jumped up and down, collecting my money. Though I paid for it for days, vomiting and lying in bed, it was worth it – showing those air force boys that an Aussie girl can drink.

By now, I had been seeing James a bit more. He told me he was willing to go to Australia with me to a make a new start, as Las Vegas was too much of a distraction for him. He said that he wanted to get his visa for Australia and to make a new life. I knew in my culture that there was no divorce, and I do believe in giving people a second chance. I could not mention this to Matt; I thought he would be saddened about the whole thing.

I had been speaking to Mum about coming home, and that it was on the cards. My sister had been diagnosed with some sort of tumour in her knee which was not malignant and was a size of a golf ball. She was making regular visits to the RPA for tests. It was mentioned that I had to come home if she needed a bone marrow transplant. I was on edge, not knowing what my sister was going through. It was her last year in high school. I thought about my ordeal, though I needed to be there for my little sister as family has always been very important to me.

With that in my mind, I was also being coached to audition for an MTV role in New York as a TV host. Rod (my radio co-host) thought this would be so amazing for me, and that was playing on my mind also.

Although a few things were now happening in my life, it was this night that I was out with Matt at Lake Mead that I will never forget. The lightning came down from afar and hit on the crystal waters, and the rain softly touched down on my face as I looked up, taking in the moon's rays. Sitting on either side of me was Phillip and William: it was great to see them again. Matt and the others were scuba-diving at night for training, and I had accompanied them. We chatted for hours, though it was William who struck a chord in me every time. He was a senior airman at twenty-one years old and just had so much potential.

'William, a guy like you should have a few girls hanging off you.'

He looked at me and smiled, then looked at the lake. He mentioned that work was his life; I told him he needed to live a bit and go enjoy life. Work would always be there; especially when you were so good at what you do. He looked at me, and it was that look that I will never forget. It was like he was at peace with himself.

Soon enough, the boys came out of the water and we all just sat there and enjoyed the rest of the night, sitting there watching the show of lightning over Lake Mead.

A few days passed, and one night I woke up from a bad dream – so bad that Dianne came running to my room and thought someone had broken in. It was 4 September 1998 and I was sweating. I had dreamed that the friends I was with that night at Lake Mead had died in a crash. It felt so real that it bothered me all morning. I remember seeing William laying on the ground in my dream and then it went black …

I parked my car and was making my way to Stash Clothing. I could see in the distance what looked like Matt standing outside the shop, in full uniform. My heart sank, then it started racing. Matt was looking pale. Dianne ran out of the store, looking at me like she was about to say sorry.

'Emily is on the phone.' I grabbed the phone from Dianne, who mentioned that she had called ten times looking for me.

'I am so sorry, Silvana.'

I could see Matt still standing there outside the store. 'Emily, I have to go, Matt is outside.'

'I'm so sorry, Silvana. Please call me later ... Please.'

I hung up the phone; my worst nightmare had come true. I ran outside and grabbed Matt and looked at him. Tears rolled down his eyes. He was in full uniform and I knew someone had died.

I grabbed him tight and hugged him; I was not much good at showing emotions, though I had to hold on to him. I opened my eyes, I could see people in the mall, standing and looking, and some had taken their hats off, while others just put their hand on their heart, to show a sign of respect for the fallen airmen. News had spread fast that morning around Las Vegas. I even got a phone call from my mother saying she heard what happened and gave her condolences to Matt.

Matt lost twelve of his friends from the squadron 66 mission in the early morning of 4 September 1998. Two Blackhawks that were in training at night had crashed due to high winds, one after the other in the Las Vegas mountains. The two men I shared talks and laughs: Phillip and William. I will never forget the night William looked at me, as if it was like a goodbye.

The funeral and memorial was held for the twelve men. It was a private function, so I could not go. In the weeks to come, things in Las Vegas were very solemn. Then one day I called Mum, thinking I was going to hang up because it was Dad that answered the phone, saying hello to me like nothing had happened. I spoke to him and he passed the phone to Mum. I told Mum I was coming home. I was bringing James with me, to give our marriage a second chance, and because of Mum and my sister. My mother had suffered a breakdown, due to me. I had been in the middle of putting my tapes together and audition for the hosting of MTV New York, where I was going to send my tape and see how my luck went. I knew that if anything happened to my mother I would not know how I would handle it.

The decision was made: I was going home and giving my marriage to James a second chance. I believe that we as humans we all make mistakes and you should have a second chance.

Though I paid in a big way for the mistake of taking him back. I hurt the person I should not have: Matt. I handled things really badly because I was scared.

I left Las Vegas in October 1998, not telling Matt that my estranged husband was coming back with me. I only said that I was going back because of Mum. He was upset about the sudden decision that I took. Though after the death of Phillip and William, I knew how important it was to go home and comfort my mother and sister. I lied to the one person I should not have. I was afraid of losing him and so kept things close to my heart.

'Out of your vulnerabilities, will come your strength.'

Boxing

Back in Australia: A Second Chance

'A second chance does not always mean a happy ending. Sometimes, it's a chance to end things right.'

— Unknown

I was back home, and my mother and sister were over the moon to see me. Dad was a man that never said sorry to me when he was wrong, though his way of showing things – allowing James and myself to live downstairs – was a sorry from him.

I tried to settle back in at Guilford, though it was hard. I felt different to my other friends, and the social acceptance and how things ran back in Las Vegas was ahead of Sydney by far.

I had come from glitter, glam and hotels the size three football fields where people were so friendly. I had a family back in Las Vegas. I had an opportunity with heading into the entertainment industry, though I needed a second chance for my family and making amends with James.

Within a week of arriving, I got a job as a casual at Parramatta Westfield, working in a ladies' fashion store. At the time, it was at its prime and was well known with the trendsetters in fashion.

James had to wait and get his permanent residency. In that time, Mum and Dad threw us a party for our wedding and to welcome us back. I worked to pay the bills and showed James around Sydney, introducing him to my friends and going back to the local venues that I used to frequent around Parramatta. James was adjusting to the way of life and culture that I had introduced him to, both Lebanese and Australian.

Matt was now writing to me every week, but I just could not tell him that my estranged husband had come back with me. I told my mother and sister about the situation; they were both understanding, though it's a decision I had to make – whether to stay with James or not. It was not nice that I was stringing Matt along, though I did have feelings for him – ones I really did not have with James. With Matt, it was different. He wrote poems to me and when he wrote to me it was from his heart. I would have pages from him, and he even sent a necklace that was made for me of my name in Arabic. He sent it over from Turkey while he served there. I still keep it to remind me of what I had and as a reminder to never be ashamed of my heritage. It was the tattoo on my left ankle that he had organised to be made into a pendant.

I made the best of my life back in Australia; I got an audition for the Arabic radio station in Parramatta, though I was given a chance working the midnight shift, reading the news. James was not happy about the situation, that I was being independent and wanting to work three nights a week and during the day. My family were happy, though I was told that I needed to stay by my husband's side and keep him happy: it's not in our culture for a woman to do things if the husband is not happy. I'm not like anyone else. This girl needed to fly and spread her wings – I was not your traditional Lebanese woman, I had become very open-minded with life, especially after living by myself in the States. I kept telling my family that I really did not care about what people think. I was sick and tired of being told how I should live my life.

Remember: in life, whether from family, friends or workmates, there are plenty of people out there who have something to say and sometimes it's not always the best advice for you. You've got to do what's best for you and you only. I learnt the hard way that you can't live your life for everyone else. As I mentioned before, being an Australian–Lebanese woman growing up when I did was a very hard time. Do what is best for you; I believe that James did not want me to fly and spread my wings. He was trying so hard to put his thumb down on me.

I did a few guest shows on 2RDJ, a community radio station in Burwood, about my life in Las Vegas and working on radio. I missed my friends back home that I was keeping in touch with postcards and phone calls.

By now, James had a job working in a local pub in Merrylands, as he got his permanent residency – though he was getting into pot again and I was being pressured to smoke it too.

Matt was now calling the house. One day, Dad answered the phone. After I got off the phone, he mentioned to me in a very stern voice that I was married and that no man should be calling me. My father did some damage to my relationship with Matt. I found out later, as my sister and I were in the back seat of the car going to a wedding, that my father had exchanged words with Matt that day and told him that I was still married and to leave me alone. My father held that information from me for four years. At the time, I did not know why the letters stopped coming or why Matt never returned my calls. I thought that something had happened to him on a mission. It took four years for me to find out, because Dad had slipped-up in the car and it came out about why Matt had cut his ties from me. There was no other means of getting in contact with him, as there was no Facebook or Twitter. Instead, it was a phone call or letter writing or email to explain and say how sorry I was. I hurt him in a terrible way, while my father intervened instead of allowing me to explain. I could have been with him, as I left James just months after the phone conversation between my father and Matt.

I felt awful, for what I did, and I never got to say that I was sorry; I tried for many years to find him on social media to apologise for what I did and explain, with no luck. I never forgave Dad for what he did and things with Dad again got worse.

James was doing late shifts at the pub and would finish at 12 pm, though he would be walking in the door at 6 am while I was getting up for work. It was happening almost every day. I would question him, as most of the time he was high on pot. The only answer I got back was that he was hanging out with friends from the pub. One day, Mum came up to me because Dad could not and told me that James and I needed to move out and work on the relationship without any interference from family. So we moved into a two-bedroom unit in Merrylands and I told James it was time for him to find a new job with better hours, hoping this would take him away from the people he was hanging with.

By now, I was 2IC (second in command) at the ladies' fashion store and decided I needed to do something for myself and took up classes at a gym in Merrylands. They had just brought boxing classes into Australia and I was so far ahead with what they were teaching. I welcomed the classes. James had taken up a job at Kings Cross on the front desk at a major hotel. I was truly happy for him, though yet again he was getting home later and later and, on some occasions, he never came home. I was sure that he was getting preoccupied, as any women would fear. So one night I went out with him, as he was going to a private party at Edgecliff with his fellow workmates, getting drunk and doing drugs. I had a few drinks, though I was observant of who and what was going on around me and the body language with some of his workmates. I was suspicious of one of his mates. James was obviously on his best behaviour while I was around.

James was starting to get into a depression and I tried every way I could to help him; he was falling into the same patterns like he was in Las Vegas. I was suffocated by him: he was never happy and it affected me, as I was always trying to do right by everyone and be positive. I threw myself into the boxing classes.

One night, when there were at least twenty-five people in the class, the ex-boxer that was taking the classes did not show up. People were getting a bit disgruntled, but as I stood back, an idea came to me: I could teach this class. I ran out to the front desk and spoke to the gym co-ordinator, explaining to her that I could do this. I did not have any certificates in fitness, there were paying customers and I wanted to help. She was desperate and took my offer. I didn't want money; I was happy to help. So I went back, with my heart skipping a beat and explained to the class – some were not happy that I was a female teaching boxing.

During the hour of the class, the gym coordinator had come past to see how I was going. When the class finished, and the clients thanked me and asked when I was teaching again. I smiled, saying I hoped it was soon. When I came up to the front desk, the coordinator smiled at me and said that she wanted to take me on.

'You had excellent feedback. I'd like you to do your Certificate III and come back to me. I want to put you on.'

So I did. I worked full-time and studied at night and juggled James. This time, I was not going to stop doing something because someone was insecure. James had come up with an idea that we should check out the Gold Coast and think about moving up there. I agreed to check it out and to introduce him to my family and godfather living there. I was not sure why James was wanting to move up the Gold Coast, but I took everything in and observed his motivation.

We ended up going on a short break to the Gold Coast and looking at areas that he would love to live. He mentioned that he wanted to start a family with me. I mentioned that was impossible, when our relationship was showing cracks. Having a baby was not going to solve anything, as he was unstable.

When we came back a few weeks later, James had got a job at the Gold Coast, in one of the hotels. He never discussed it with me, and I thought it was a phase. But it was not, and I was moving to the Gold Coast. I thought, yet again, that maybe this would help the marriage. He moved up first, leaving me to deal with the furniture and everything else. It was such a quick move for him. Something in me was saying this did not feel right and being by myself had made me think things through in a logical way. I thought about why James never had mail come to the unit and the night we had gone out to Edgecliff and his nights not coming home.

I went to the Merrylands Post Office and asked if James had a PO Box. As I had a different surname to his, the person that was looking after me actually gave me the key. Back then it was easy to get your partner's details, and it was not so much of a security risk, like it is now. I opened it up and found bills addressed to him. We both shared a joint credit card. Thoughts went through my head. I got a second key from the post office.

I kept tabs on the mail coming in. I had bills being racked up on my credit card and I never knew why because I never got the statements. Though there it was: I was being billed for hotel rooms and also a phone bill had come in at $3000. I didn't get angry; I kept to my existing plan.

I researched the calls – they were being made to a 1300 sex number. I called the phone company and argued with them. They ended up not charging me, as my surname was different to James' and it was in his name. I said that this person never lived at this address. Everything was in my name: the unit and every other bill that we had to pay, except the joint credit card. How dumb was he to do what he did on a joint credit card!

I was not angry; I gave him a second chance. I was not there to get even; I was there to get my life back. James called me most nights and I pretended everything was fine. He mentioned a few times that his flatmate had brought escorts to the unit. I'm not like most women; I did not fly off the handle: I was going to handle this in a diplomatic way. Yelling was not going to get me anywhere, so I listened as he kept mentioning how desperate he was, and I could tell in his voice he was high again and that he was not happy.

A few nights passed, and he called to say that the credit card was not working for him. I mentioned I could not pay the bill and he had to make amends on his own. He also asked when I was moving. I said that I was not moving to the Gold Coast: I was staying in Sydney and I could not do this anymore. I wanted to file for a divorce. He got angry and said that he was just with me so that he could get a visa and get into the country. He laughed over the phone and thanked me.

I confided in my mother and my sister what had happened and my decision. Dad lost his cool and said that we do not have women in our family who were divorced – you would be the first and people will look at you differently. Again: I knew I was not here to live for others – it was *my* happiness.

I lashed out at him.

'I got married to escape you, and I wanted happiness in my life!' I wanted to live without his constant putting me down and embarrassing him and the family, as for him life was all about that. At this stage, I wanted to go back to Las Vegas. I just could not live in this culture; I was different. I always felt alone in the world and thought I just didn't fit in because of other people's way of thinking.

There was a knock on the door and I opened it to see James. He stormed in and threatened to take everything.

'Sure, you can have whatever you want. I really do not care.'

He wanted to know why I was doing this, and I explained the bills and the money he owed on the credit card. He came back with how he was alone and needed to fill a hole. I mentioned the visa thing and how I should have listened to my heart back in Vegas when he mentioned it the first time. I explained how he tried to stop me from being happy and every time I found happiness in something he would always try to take it away from me.

'You forget James that you did not do nice things in Vegas and I tried many times to help. You say you're lonely, though I felt the same in Vegas, though the difference between you and me is that I did something about it – even when I was faced with a health scare. I got up and decided to take charge of my life even when you tried to side-track me with pot smoking and heavy drinking and not working. You got upset because my circle of friends was expanding. You had insecurity issues, and I was not going to let that bring me down.'

'I tried so hard, but I just don't love you, and I never did. You were my first in everything and I thank you that you opened my eyes to see things in a different light. I do not hate you; I need to move on and protect myself.'

He gathered his things and left, without saying a word.

I had gone to legal aid with my mother, to see what rights I had with a marriage that had taken place in Vegas. I was in luck: my marriage was not recognised here, as I was not registered and I had my surname. All I needed was the divorce papers sent from Vegas. I would be divorced in one month, due to the Vegas laws.

James was making it hard on me and would call and threaten me most nights. I decided that I would speak to immigration and work on getting James out of my life. I wrote a letter to not to become a sponsor anymore for James and let them know that I was no longer living with him.

Immigration responded and revoked his permanent status. The last I heard was that his father came and took him back to the States. Two months later, my divorce papers came through to sign and send back. A note was left on it saying that he was not sure why I left him. I didn't respond, as he thought that I was naive enough to stay with him, because of my culture. If anything, James, you made me closer to becoming stronger. You gave me more independence and helped me find what I wanted to be and how I wanted to live. I do not hate you: I thank you. And that was the last I heard from my ex-husband.

'Never make someone a priority when all you are to them is an option.'

MAYA ANGELOU

Renaissance

Dark Times

'Life
Has knocked me down a few times. It has shown me things I never wanted to see. I have experienced sadness and failures. But one thing for sure …
I ALWAYS GET UP.'

— Unknown

I moved back home, with Dad trying to put some house rules on me like I was back in high school. I was getting used to living back home but Dad didn't want any of my friends to visit. This was like a joke, I just needed to get back on my feet before I moved out again; I respected that it was his home.

One day, I was sitting at Ridges chatting with a mate that I had not seen in a long time. He was doing security work there and Bill walked past, pushing his toddler in a pram. He looked like death. Now, there is history with Bill and me, but it had been years since I saw him last. We used to always hang out, and he had been a very close friend of mine who I had known since high school, along with Michael, who I had known since I was born. These were the only males Dad allowed me to hang out with while I was growing up.

Bill would always take me on his motor bike up to Kurrajong, where the views were spectacular. We would sit for hours and talk and there were times we would just sit there and not talk at all. You know that feeling, when you're with someone and you're that comfortable that you know each other's thoughts, or you're happy with the company, that words are not needed. It was like that with us all the time. He loved to ride, and I enjoyed being in his company. He owned his own takeaway shop by the age of twenty-one and I thought he was beyond his years. My parents and his family, being Lebanese, thought there was marriage on the cards for us. No-one could understand that you could have friends from the opposite sex.

I had packed my bags and took off overseas, and while I didn't hear much from Bill until I got back, he had got married and had twins. I was happy for him; he had distanced himself from me due to the wife, and I understood. Friendships change when you have a partner who does not understand. I was married to James when I came home, and I told James of the male friends I had in my life and that were close to me. I always mentioned this to guys I was dating; a few were OK with it though there were plenty that that were not. I always took the second option and walked away from them. I have more than forty years of friendship with a male friend; there's no way I have to stop that because of gender. I do not think someone can tell me who to be friends with when I have only known them for five minutes. It showed me their character and I knew I would not last with them, so I walked away sometimes and that suited me fine.

It was such a shock when after we'd lost contact for a few years, there was Bill walking past me like a ghost out of the blue. He walked past me and looked straight through me. I was in shock and I couldn't make the words come out to say hello, He looked like a mess.

A few months later, I was at work and my mother called me to come home straight away. I knew there was something wrong. I found out from Bill's aunty, there at my parents' house, that Bill had committed suicide. They wanted to know if I had seen him or heard from him, and I explained I had seen him. He had gassed himself in Lithgow in his car. The next day he was found by a cyclist. I was shattered; he left behind his wife and twins. I didn't know what was going on with him; he was a hardworking man and was loved by many.

I remember going to pay my respects to his family and his grandmother had grabbed me in tears, looking at me, saying to me in Arabic, 'Of all the people he knew, you would have known if something was wrong with him.'

I explained that I had been out of the country for some years and that I had seen him just once in the street in Parramatta when I came back. That he had walked past me like a ghost but he really hadn't stopped to chat with me. I had known there was something wrong then.

A few years later, my close friend Michael lost his twenty-three-year-old brother to a drunken driver. It made me realise how important life is, and how short it is. It's up to us to be around people that are not toxic and to do the things we really want to do in life.

So I started going out and making a new circle of friends. It's funny, once your circumstances change, like getting a divorce, you are surround by a different group of people. By now, my social group was quite diverse.

My relationship with my father reached breaking point when I brought a male friend back home one night. By the next day, Dad was in a rage and yelled at me to get out of the house, saying that I had disgraced him, knowing I had a younger sister at home. So with just the clothes on my back and my handbag, I left. It took me a day to find a place to live. I had just met a girl, name Connie, who had a spare room in Blacktown and she took me in. I managed to grab my clothing from my parents' place when Dad was not there.

I settled in; she was quite independent and not much older than me. She would take me with her almost every weekend horse riding, as she had two horses. I had found a passion for riding and I learnt so much with her. We even started going to the races, as this was all new to me – but I loved it. She was filled with confidence and I would watch her work her way around the room – men loved her, and you could see why they did.

My drinking started to get the better of me; I would drive home drunk at times. I really did not know how I got home: I was really lucky. I am glad that I got over that phase. I guess it was the only way that I knew of dealing with Bill's death. Sometimes, I feel that he was around in my darkest time and that I had an angel looking out for me.

Connie sat me down one evening and asked me what I wanted for my present life. I mentioned that I wanted to own my first home. I now was working full-time at a clothing store and was only on $38,000 a year as a 2IC.

It was the year 2000 and I wanted to come into the new year with a goal. Connie mentioned that it could happen, and that she would organise a broker to come over and chat with me and see what we could do.

The broker came over a week later and chatted with me. I was going to get my home, if I stayed within a certain price range. As the first home buyer's grant was $14,000, and stamp duty was free, I had a chance – though it was hard for a single female on my wage to get a home back then. It was going to happen: Connie had opened the door for me. I had no idea about entering the housing market and Connie was going to help me make it happen.

The light had started appearing through those grey clouds.

One night when I was out with Connie and her friends at the Argyle in Parramatta, I met a gentleman – physically strong and over six foot tall. We connected and it was great to chat with him. I was starting to get into doing more fitness classes and he would be competing for the kickboxing titles overseas in Asia in a few months' time; I was quite impressed.

He asked me out and I was not too sure, though the girls that were with us that night said I had nothing to lose. He was quite cute, I thought. He lived way out west, and I never thought twice about picking him up – maybe because I trusted him and believe everyone has a good character and that I had nothing to fear. He told me that he didn't have a car due to being overseas most of the year.

He decided that the two of us should head to the beach. I was wearing a short denim skirt and a white shirt. I should have realised that the beach was not a safe environment for me.

The next thing I remember was been grabbed violently and then thinking I was not strong enough. I could not keep my attacker off me. It was over in a few shocking minutes. I just could not believe what had just happened to me. I was numb. I vaguely remember dropping him off home and drove off. I was in shock and didn't want to believe that this had happened to me. This was date rape; I do not remember saying yes – if anything, I had screamed but there was no-one around, no-one to hear my cries. I cried all the way home. I was ashamed of what had happened, and I wanted the ground to open up right there and swallow me. I got home, and Connie was still up. She knew something was up. I went into the shower and scrubbed for over an hour until I was red raw on my skin.

I got out, wiped the mirror and looked at myself, with make-up running down my face. This night changed me as a person. I kept looking in the mirror; I was not going to allow another man to touch me again, unless it was with my consent. The world was not filled with roses and there are people who are evil. I was lucky. I prayed in the bathroom. I was alive; he hadn't killed me. I believe my friend Bill, my guardian angel, had looked after me and made sure I got out of there.

There is a God.

A few weeks later, I had been feeling sick and I made sure I threw out the clothes, shoes and my handbag that reminded me of that night.

I never went to the police, as I was so worried about my parents, my father and the disgrace that I as a daughter would bring upon my family; I kept quiet. But I had to speak to someone, and my flatmate Connie was the next best thing. I told her what had happened and she was in disbelief. She heard that the guy had left the country and it made sense. I also explained that I was feeling ill. She feared the worst and went out and got me a pregnancy test. I went into the toilet to use the test and came back with tears in my eyes. I had fallen pregnant to my rapist; this just got worse.

'What are you going to do Silvana? You cannot keep the pregnancy.'

'No, I cannot keep a pregnancy and bring up a child and explain how they were conceived. In our culture, we do not believe in having sex before marriage. Can you imagine me telling my parents that I have to have an abortion? I will definitely have no family in the future, as I am struggling now with my own family.'

'We'll organise to take you to a clinic and get this sorted.'

Connie organised everything for me. She came into my life at the right time – I believe that people come into your life for a reason or as a lesson; she was there for my dark time.

If you know anyone that has been in a similar situation, my advice is to seek help, get the police involved and get counselling. I didn't do that; instead, I became destructive and did not deal with it properly. It was only years later that I went to see a councillor, though by then I had dealt with what had happened.

Wonderwoman!

Saving My Life and Competing In Ms Fitness/Ms East Coast

'The best protection any woman can have ... is courage.'

— Elizabeth Cady Stanton

I was regaining my life back – or trying to. For a while that event haunted me. I needed to refocus, and I ended buying a property in Merrylands West: a two-bedroom apartment that needed a bit of fixing up. The gentleman who sold it had just been through a divorce and had sold the unit for a steal at $156,000. I remember taking the keys off the agent, and there I was in the living room. I fell to the ground and cried – not of sadness but of joy. I was not going to be a victim; I was going to be a fighting spirit. No matter what challenges came my way, I was going to tackle things head on. I was going to be even stronger mentally and physically and appreciate what I had around me.

I had to go and do a check-up with a pap smear, which came back positive; I was in a state of shock. What now? Another challenge. There is a virus called HPV which can lead to cervical cancer if not treated. This virus has come and gone through most of my life: I have had four surgeries to my cervix. Because of that, each time my cervix got smaller and weaker. This came to haunt me in my forties. I can't stress enough the need to be careful when being sexually active, as men who have HPV do not usually show visible signs and probably do not know they are carrying it. I had CNN stage 3, and within a month of finding this out I was admitted for day surgery and the bad skin tissues where taken out of my cervix, to prevent cancer from developing. Years later a vaccine came out, though for me it was too late. I always stress to my friends that they should always get a pap smear; it might save your life.

I did not give myself enough time for recovery. I threw myself back into the gym and was teaching box-fit classes five times a week and working full-time. I never mentioned that a month before my surgery I had an abortion. I was embarrassed and did not want to relive the events. It turned out that I had internal bleeding and if it was not for my sister rushing me to hospital, well, I would not be writing this story now.

I had to take over a month off work and not do anything, just to recover from pushing myself and not listening to my body when it was crying out for rest.

In that time, my father had come over to my place with my brother. My mother had given me a heads up that he wanted to see what I had bought and wanted to help with fixing a few things up.

It was pretty weird when I opened the door: as I had been in the middle of painting and then I had stopped everything due to my health. He never said sorry, he just looked around then picked up the paintbrush and asked me where I was up to and continued. It was his way of making peace. My brother and dad helped out a lot and soon the unit was looking more like a home.

'You know what Silvana, no matter what happens to you and what comes at you, you survive. I could throw you in the gutter and you would pick yourself back up.'

That coming out of Dad's mouth was nothing but a huge boost to my damaged confidence. I was never one to show my feelings and emotions. I kept quiet about the events I had been through. My family did not need to know the details of what happened. I was happy in the moment, I never gave up, and I pushed myself even after what had happened.

I felt there, in that moment and in the future, I was able to take on anything and anyone that came up and anything that challenged me in any way.

Never allow anyone to put you down and undermine you in any way. We are all equals and this was going to be my shining point very soon.

'Life's not about how hard of a hit you can give. It's about how many you can take, and still keep moving forward.'

— Rocky Balboa

I was back at the gym training and teaching classes soon enough. I asked one of the trainers, Amy, about competing, as I saw her going through a routine with two other clients. She looked at me and told me that there was a lot of dedication in competing. There was a look in her eyes that told me she thought I could not take it.

I mentioned it was my first time competing and I needed guidance for preparation. I have never lifted heavy weights or knew much about them. Amy took me on board and watched me develop; she was amazed at how my body took to weights. It took me three months and I lost twelve kilograms, weighing in at fifty-nine kilos of nothing but lean muscle. I was at twelve percent body fat and I could not drop any more weight, as I would be looking really lean. I worked hard, my diet was very strict and everything had to be measured. I trained five days a week and in the last month before competing I was doing cardio twice a day: in the morning before work and in the evening after teaching class. I was working full-time and teaching five classes and juggling training.

There were many people who had something negative to say about my healthy eating and question my reasons for doing this to my body. I had to cover up all the time at the gym, as everyone had to whisper, or I got asked if I was taking steroids. My body was in such form that the trainer asked me to cover up at training, so I was not being affected by the comments. It affected me at work, though; as I was always on my feet selling and my energy levels were all over the place. But I was determined to do this for me. I wanted to push my body to the limits. People who are always negative about things that you do are either insecure or know nothing about those things. I wanted to do this for me, after what happened to me. I was not going to be a victim: I was going to make my own stances and capture my life back.

The day before the competition, I had my little army of my brother and Michael come up, as I prepared myself with my routine. My small red bikini, red shoes, tanned skin, hair and nails were all in check. I was ready: I was going on stage to compete, and I was not here to win. I was already a winner, just by doing this.

The day came; I was surprised by my workmates who drove up the coast to see me. I was honoured to have them come: my little army grew. All the females came on stage flexing and posing for the panel of judges. I remember walking out and smiling to the judges and looking over to see my little army cheering. Then the competitors had to do individual performances in front of everyone. I had mine to Destiny's Child 'Bootylicious'. My trainer had picked the song for me, as it was appropriate to the way my figure was looking.

I came out and did the performance with my heart, not thinking much of it until we had to come out and the winners were called out. Third place was called, then second place and then first place for the 2001 Ms East Coast Australia was called out.

I heard my name.

I just stood there for a few seconds as I realised I had won the competition in my division. I was given a bunch of flowers and a trophy. What just happened? My trainer ran up to me and hugged me; her look was different now, and she knew that I had been the underdog and that no-one saw me coming from the dark into the light.

It was celebrations for a week; my brother showed me the video on VCR – it was before DVDs came out. I laughed, as Michael had to grab the video camera off him, as my brother could not film me anymore. All I could hear on the video was, 'I cannot film my sister: she is in a bikini and she looks amazing,' and the camera dropped.

In just over a week, I was competing again in the first ever Ms Fitness NSW. This was the first time Ms Fitness came to Australia and because of how well the event went from that, Ms Fitness is still in the Australasian Natural Bodybuilding (ANB) and the scene has been set for other fitness competitors in NSW.

The day came when I was feeling nervous, and this time I had most of the gym come, as we had three females competing from our gym. I also had my mother and father: this was a special event for me - having my father there. It meant so much to me, after years of struggle I was starting to see a changed man, who was willing to adapt to the strength of his daughter and accept that I was who I was.

So it was held at the Bankstown Sport Centre on 23 September 2001 and there were over 800 people. I ate a Big Mac before going on stage, as it would be a highly charged, two-minute fitness routine and I needed a boost. Amy, my trainer, had picked J-Lo's *Let's get loud*, and though we had the song speeded up, it sounded amazing. I was wearing a Wonder Woman outfit, shorts and a sports bikini top. I still get called Wonder Woman by my closest friends, because of that day. This lioness was ready to roar and show the crowd what fitness was all about. I came on stage with a force and out of the crowd all I could see was my parents waving and smiling and calling my name. I went for it with the kicks, the punches and one-arm push ups. I had a great attitude with this routine – I wanted to win the judges and the crowd. I smiled right through and was confident in my moves. I finished looking at the crowd, roaring for more, and Mum and Dad were standing and calling my name. I had tears falling down my face as I was happy. I had taken on a challenge and I had hit it face-on, with my father watching.

Competitors came out for each division, and then our division came and I was standing there, looking at my parents. I was not thinking of winning: I had already won, just having my father there, knowing that he had come there for me. I didn't care about the past. We deal with challenges and overcome them and eventually forgive, especially when it comes to family; that's all that mattered to me. Like last time, they called out third place, second place and then the winner of the 2001 Ms Fitness NSW contest.

'Ms Fitness NSW 2001, the first time for this division to come to Australia for the ANB Federation. A week after previously winning Ms East Coast Australia!'

The whole place was on its feet; my trainer came up and grabbed me, she was just amazed at my achievement. If she only knew what I had gone through in that year. I was handed a trophy that stood up to my thigh. I looked at the trophy, it was of an angel holding her arms up in Victory. This was for all the challenges I had faced in the past. There I was: anything was possible.

I had a small write-up in *Ironman* magazine, along with my fellow teammates a few months later. Our photos were displayed in the gym and the weirdest thing was that the heavy, so-called 'bad boys' at the gym – the ones you would not approach – came to me one by one and thanked me for doing the gym proud and putting it and the Lebanese community on the map. Most of them were also of Lebanese background and it was not every day you saw a female of Lebanese background competing.

I had broken the stereotype.

'I am a fighter
I will fight for what I want and what I love until the end of time
Never Give up
Never back down.'

— UNKNOWN

My journey

Alternative Path

'Your Journey
has molded you for your greater good and it was exactly what it needed to be.
Don't think you've lost time ... it took each and every situation you have encountered to bring you to the now. And the now is right on time.'

— Asha Tyson

After my winning events, I became bulimic. I couldn't handle the intake of food and was vomiting after gorging. After one week of competing, I gained ten kilos. My body was conserving all the food I was consuming. I started to feel a bit down on myself. I had no guidance from my trainer, Amy, and it took almost a year to get my body back on track. I put myself on a diet plan for healthy eating and would make regular trips to health food stores and started seeing a naturopath. I eventually felt better.

After what I went through to get my health back and finally getting my period back after a year of losing it, I just didn't want to compete anymore. I had also been working three jobs full-time: at the women's clothing store as a store manager and winning the small business awards for the Parramatta district, teaching five box-fit classes a week, and also on Friday and Saturday nights as a trainee security guard at Revesby Workers Club where I was dealing with the worst people that could gather at one venue. I had been subject to manhandling men and breaking-up physical fights, attending women vomiting in toilets and dealing with male co-workers who hated the thought that I was working with them, because I was a female in a male's job. I could handle myself in many situations, and was able to end them with a positive outcome. But it was getting too much: what I was seeing, walking through the dance floor keeping an eye out for trouble, the calls I would get from patrons, and the ones that tried to pick me up every weekend. I maintained a very cool professional attitude.

I remember one night, I had to be on the podium as it was the best way to keep an eye on the crowd. There were three other security guards as the crowd had turned and become aggressive. Glass bottles and punches were being thrown, and the four of us had to jump down to break-up the fight. It was pretty scary, as I had pulled off one of the guys who I saw throw a bottle and tried to put him in a head lock. I could not hold on to him for long though, but soon help had arrived and police were on the scene. I took a step back after everything settled. I went up to my manager and said that I could not do this anymore and I quit. I had to think of my safety, and each weekend was like walking into a lion's den. A year later, the manager walked into the fashion store I was working in and wanted me back, as he loved my work ethic. It just was not my path, I explained to him.

So I applied for various government jobs: I needed a change in my life. I was at a crossroads again and working three jobs and paying off a mortgage. I applied for over forty jobs around 2001. I knew because of what happened to me in the States that my surname was the problem; the Gulf War had such an effect on people due to having a tyrant like Saddam Hussein in the Middle East. I was not related to him in any way but I still cut my hair short and dyed it blonde.

I applied for the air force, to be part of a flight attended crew, and I got through all my admin and interviews but pulled my application out before going any further. My case manager, for the air force, insisted I stay and see it through, but I could not do it for what they were offering at the time, as I had to pay off a mortgage, and I had no help; as usual, I was looking after myself.

On another occasion, I applied for a flight attendant's role with an airline. I was knocked back due to the Arabic tattoo on my ankle. I got through to the third stage but then they asked me if there were any tattoos visible, and that's how far my application went, because I bared ink on my body. I applied to be in the on-call fire brigade for my area and was selected from the 140 applications. I was standing in front of a panel of four interviewers at my local fire station but I didn't get through, though I was happy I got that far.

That was when I applied for the police force. It was my new dream as I wanted to help my community and prove the haters wrong: that women and people of my heritage can do right. I passed all the administration tests, receiving admirable recommendations from an associate that I knew – a sergeant in the police force – and another who was in the senate in parliament. I passed all security checks and medical tests. I received a letter saying that I had qualified for the fitness test in Goulbourn; I was so excited. I dyed my hair back to its natural colour and thought, I'm not going to hide and be something that I am not.

It was a big day; I was here at the Academy and we were being drilled. The officer in charge was yelling at us and a few in the group were taking it as a joke. I felt like I was in the army. I had been flying through all my tests until I came across a female trainer. She spoke to me quite rudely as I was doing my sit-up test. With my feet still planted on the ground and holding my core in, as I came up and held my position for a few seconds. She told me that I had failed and that she could not look at me. When she said that, I looked at her and got up in disbelief.

'On what grounds have you failed me? I did that correctly!'

At the time, I was working as a fitness instructor five days a week, teaching five classes, and I knew I had nailed that.

'Are you answering me back? You've failed.'

I knew I had to walk away; by failing one part of the test I had failed my entire test. I went back to the head trainer and told him what had just happened. He looked very surprised. He said that he should not say anything to her and that I had to put this in as a formal complaint if I thought I had been looked at unfairly.

Just like that, I failed. I cried all the way from Goulbourn to Guildford. I wanted to see my mother. I was embarrassed: here I was, teaching and competing in fitness, and I had failed. I could not show my face to my workmates, family and friends. This hit me pretty hard, and it took me weeks to get over what had happened.

A few weeks later, I was working as a casual in Bardot, one of the happening women's fashion stores in Parramatta, and two police officers walked in, asking for me. I was in the back room doing stock and my manager at the time thought I was in trouble – just typical thinking. I came out, and was taken outside the store. They had heard what had happened with me and had reviewed my files. They were from the recruitment office in Parramatta. They both mentioned that my file was outstanding and that they wanted more people like me in the police force. They said the trainer had failed a few more females and that she was under investigation. They wanted me to re-sit my fitness test.

I declined: if this was going to be how I got treated, what was it going to be like for me in there? I had been discriminated against. I thanked the two officers for coming to try and change my mind. There is a reason for everything, and it was not my path. The recruitment office tried for another six months to get me back but I just ignored their communications and moved on with my life. I kept the paperwork for years – I couldn't let go until late in 2015 when I was going through all my files and I finally threw them out.

I was determined; I was not going to stop. I applied for ASIO, as I had responded to an ad that they were looking for a diverse range of people with skills and who could speak another language – especially Arabic. I was selected, as my paperwork had gotten through to the next level out of more than 700 applicants. I had known a federal police officer and so I was groomed for my exams and sat for them. I didn't get through; I might have slipped up, as I was not supposed to tell anyone what I was applying for, but I had mentioned it to my family. I was happy that I got the chance to be exposed to the different interviews and exams I was applying for. I know it can be disheartening and can get you down, though the jobs I was applying for were not just regular jobs. I knew I was applying for jobs that were about helping others and the country.

With working hard and having no fun, I became destructive. I was introduced to dance festivals so I could have some fun – my first was Two Tribes at Homebush. Dance events were something different back then, they were mind-blowing. I entered into a world of dance and drugs, and for years I had no regrets about doing what I did. I eventually stopped, as I knew it was affecting my life, though for that short period it helped my pain. I discovered that I could dance really well and I was often asked if I was a dancer. My friends were surprised to see this side of me; it was my outlet and I needed it.

I was always getting into fights with men. At one venue, I actually punched and knocked out one guy. He had grabbed my friend in a place he shouldn't and then grabbed me when I was ordering a drink. I turned around and punched him in his throat and he fell very hard on his back while a bartender jumped over the bar and grabbed me. He knew I wanted to finish this bastard.

After what happened to me, I was *not* going to have a male touch me again without my consent. The security guard came over and saw me in a hold from the bartender and the guy on the floor holding his throat. Well, back then no questions were asked: the guard grabbed the guy and threw him out of the club.

Years later, I had another incident. I was out with friends at a well-known bar on George Street in the city. I met a girl from England in the bathroom called AJ; she was in Sydney by herself, so I asked if she wanted to join me and my friends. Well, soon after, this guy came up to her (she was very pretty, very exotic looking) and he kept harassing her and saying things I could not believe were coming out of his mouth. I stepped in and politely told him that she was not interested and asked him to give her some space. Well, he came back with vengeance. I looked into his eyes; my gut knew this man was not safe. I spoke to him again, and although I even had males in my group of friends who could see what was happening, no-one stepped in. Then, without notice, the guy came up and spat in my face. It was horrifying. I acted quickly and grabbed him around the throat in front of all the patrons. I picked him up and flung him into a nearby column. I was going to hit him. While he was turning red, his friends jumped in, asking me to let him go. Security surrounded me, thinking it was two guys in a fight, and they were surprised it was a female grabbing a male.

I dropped him and said, 'Never judge a book by its cover. You picked the wrong person tonight to be a fucking sleaze with.'

I walked away and said my piece to my friends who had not stepped in to help. My girlfriend at the time, who was there, mentioned that I had embarrassed her at the Establishment. I didn't care, because that friendship didn't last after that; loyalty is what I am about, and helping others in a time of need.

We walked out of the venue with everyone looking and making a path for AJ and me, like it was something out of a movie. I got to the doors and one of the security guards said, 'Good on you. You showed that guy what he did was wrong.' I smiled and walked off.

AJ and I got a drink, and I found out she was a criminal lawyer and she thanked me ever so much for protecting her.

'That guy was really dangerous, if you hadn't been there ... God knows what would have happened.'

'I was there at the right time at the right place. We were meant to meet, AJ.'

We put our glasses up and toasted to friendship. I am still in contact with her even today.

I was becoming aggressive; I had anger in me when it came to some men. I also had trust issues, so I was out and about all the time with the gay community. It was my haven to be around my gay friends: I felt safe and like I was not judged. I wanted to be away from the world of fake people and men who just had no respect for women. I would go out all the time to gay clubs. I loved the music they played; it was like being in Vegas again. It was also a place where I never got harassed by straight men so I could dance on my own without being worried. Some of my friends were curious with my outings to these dance clubs – then they would come and realise how much fun it was.

I was with a friend, Jane, one time in the middle of ARQ night club, dancing and laughing.

'Do you realise something Jane? There are topless men all around us, looking so fine, and they are gay and no-one has harassed us.'

We laughed and danced for hours. ARQ became my second home for years. I just didn't like the wannabe muscle heads that came through the doors at the other venues, all trying to outdo each other in the muscle department and dance like they had just come back from a marathon. It was not my scene. ARQ suited me and my quirky friends fine. Sometimes, one of the security guards would clear the podium for me and pick me up and put me on there. I danced for the crowd that watched me from two different levels. I danced with my heart and soul and loved watching the place go off: I was in my element.

Dancing helped me express myself. One night, one of my gay friends, Sasha, wanted me to go with him to the Mardi Gras after party. This was all new to me and we organised for me to go in leather pants, leather bikini top and studded belt, with my hair braided in a tribal look. Sasha wanted me to look fierce, as it was the theme for the night. He was a hairdresser; it was handy to have him around when going out, as he made sure my hair was never out of place.

So here I was at Moore Park, walking into this event. There were people from all walks of life and the music was just spectacular. We were dancing for not even an hour when I had a tap on my shoulder from the stage staff.

'We would like you to dance in the cage please: you look and move great.'

I stood there, while my friend was pushing me to go and dance.

'OMG Silvana, you have to go up there and dance! What an honour.'

I was spotted from thousands of people dancing and they picked me. I agreed to do it. I went, and the DJ gave the signal for me to go into the cage and dance. My friend stood backstage, watching me. I was nervous entering the cage: there were thousands of people watching me. I thought to myself that I would just do it like I was dancing at ARQ. I danced, going with the beat of the music, and seduced the crowd. They wanted a show, and I gave it to them. For almost an hour I danced and entertained the crowd. At the end, they allowed my friend to come and join me. I remember getting off stage with everybody mentioning how amazing I was and asking what dance company I was from. But all I did was dance and listen to the beat. It was my outlet; I escaped by dancing and listening to the music.

'Music and dance saved my soul.'

With Kostya Tszyu

Finding My Outlet

'Your life is controlled by what you focus on.'

— Tony Robbins

I spent a few years using dance as my outlet, but knew I needed to get back to my roots. I wanted to brush-up and learn a bit more boxing. I kept going out, though my scene had changed: now I was hanging out with different social groups and the drugs were out of my system.

I ended up one day following my brother to the PCYC (Police Citizen Youth Club) fitness centre in Parramatta with my flatmate at the time. My brother was in shock when he saw me, he came up and asked me what the hell I was doing there. I wanted to do the class; the trainer looked at me, clearly thinking this desire was a passing phase for the two girls that stood in front of him.

I took the class, with my brother trying to avoid me. I had all my wraps, rope and gloves and was determined to see the class through. My flatmate ended up stepping out, as it was too much for her, but I continued. I think the guys in the gym wanted me to give up, though I didn't: I kept fighting.

Once I had finished the class, my brother had a word with me outside.

'This gym is not for you. This is a proper boxing gym.'

'Embarrassed are we, about your sister who might outdo you?'

So I continued to go to PCYC Parramatta but my brother stopped going because of me. I learnt to fight and defend. After three months the trainer knew I was serious about my training, and he called me into the ring and asked me my nickname. I knew I was accepted by him.

'Call me Sil, short for Silvana.'

Remember that women in boxing back in 2002 were rare. It was illegal for women to fight in NSW – if they wanted to fight, they had to go interstate. I trained because I wanted to brush-up and move like a dangerous weapon, in case I needed to defend myself. It also helped me with being focused in my job and in my personal life; it gave me confidence.

I trained three times a week for a year. Sometimes I would get guys from across the gym laugh at me, when I was in the ring training, because I was female. As the gym was next door to the police headquarters, a lot of police officers came in, though they never spoke to me, as I was training in a male-dominated sport. I continued with the support of gentleman named Kurt, who trained with me on the nights I came in. He wanted me to continue and ignore the ignorance I had around me.

The gentleman I trained with was a charity worker and always travelled abroad to help with building communities. We helped each other and he found it amazing that I had the courage to be in a gym filled with men and do something for myself. He said it explained a lot about my character.

'A bird sitting on a tree is never afraid of the branch breaking,
Because her trust is not on the branch but on its own wings.
Always believe in yourself.'

— Unknown

A Dangerous Relationship

'The size of your success is measured by the strength of your desire; the size of your dream; and how you handle disappointment along the way.'

— Robert T. Kiyosaki

So time went on and one night I was out with friends and met a gentleman, called Brad, that took a liking to me. He was ten years older than me. I gave him my number and thought nothing of it until a few days later when I got a phone call from him. Brad had really made an effort to go out with me, though I was not sure why he was so interested in me, as I had my walls up and kept my heart guarded.

He was a born and bred Bondi Boy and had a daughter who was three years old. I was not sure how I felt about a child being in the picture, as I could hear my parents in my ear saying that was baggage for me. But he made every effort to come and see me at Merrylands. This was all new to me: the child and an ex-wife, and so I had to deal with that also. I was half-hearted about that being in my life, as I just didn't want dramas with an ex-wife and a child. I thought that after what I had been through, the last thing I wanted was this.

But I kept an open mind, and every time I saw Brad I became closer to him. He could sense that I was proceeding cautiously with this relationship. I had been seeing him for a month when he asked me for a favour.

'Silvana, I need $10,000 from you.'

I stood there, dumbfounded.

'You are asking me in a car park. This is not appropriate. I have only known you for a month and you're asking me that.'

He was so bold and replied that I had a mortgage and I could refinance my loan for him.

'Just because I have a mortgage, does not make me a moneybags. Sorry, the answer is no, and if you're not happy I'll make it easy for you: stop seeing me.'

'Sorry I asked; I should have never asked you, Silvana.'

Though my mind kept going over what he had said, I was sure he was desperate or owed someone money. A few months later, he asked if he could move in with me. My first reaction was: you live in Bondi and you want to move to Merrylands? Yet again, I was mindful with what was going on.

He did move in, as I told my parents that I wanted to see how we lived together. My mother was very cautious, asking why someone from Bondi wanted to live in Merrylands, and reminded me of that.

Brad was settled in and things began to change. He was going out – which didn't bother me because I was not one of those women that got jealous, and I always believed that things would come out in due time. In that time, he was curious why I was training at a boxing gym and I felt he was threatened. I also decided in the time I was seeing him that I was going to have a breast augmentation, as I had no chest and felt boyish with my muscly figure. Brad was not happy I was getting this done and felt very insecure with my decision.

'I am the one paying for it with my money, so I will do what makes me happy.'

So what does a guy do to control a woman that is strong? He found my weakness and somehow came across cocaine like it was so in fashion and I was offered it all time. Slowly, he was getting me to break down my walls and get me when I was vulnerable. He felt the need for me to want him and be dependent on him – and slowly, it worked. It got to the point that I was taking drugs at work. I even stopped going to boxing and I started to lose weight fast.

I had always had a feeling that Brad was involved in serious illicit drugs. My worst fears came to life one day in the summer of 2004. When I was putting away bedsheets in my bedroom, I noticed a hole the size of a fifty-cent piece. My heart sunk. I looked closer: it was a hidden camera. I pulled it right out, cord and all.

We were being filmed and it made me sick. I called my mother. She had kept telling me that the man I was with was not safe and he was dangerous. I called Brad and told him what I had just found. At first he thought I was making this up, then he realised from my voice that I was not. He was home after that really fast. I mentioned that I wanted to call the police, as this violated our privacy. He begged me not to and said he would call his stepfather (who was in the police force) to sort it out.

'No: I want police here that do not know you. You can call your stepfather and advise him of what's happened.'

The police came over; there was about a dozen officers in the unit. The sergeant who was there said that a few women in the area who lived on their own were being filmed. I mentioned that I was living with my boyfriend and this was all too weird. He asked me to tape up all vents with black plastic and cover around the light fittings.

They took my statement and left. Brad was scratching his head. He was nervous and moved around the unit. After that I could not sleep for days.

What the hell had I gotten myself into? I knew that I was in way over my head. I knew leaving this relationship with him was going to take planning.

'Silvana, we are moving from here. I found a place in Vaucluse, a two-bedroom unit on the water.'

'So, Brad, we are going to your area now?'

'Yes, we are.'

Our plans were delayed due to me going into hospital again for the second surgery on my cervix. I had to stop work, as I could not recover properly. I told my parents that we were moving, and my mother was so upset. I kept telling her that I would still be here in Sydney: I was not going overseas.

We moved to the eastern suburbs. I fitted in, as I had my hair short and a lot of people in the area of Vaucluse thought that I was Jewish. Going to the local shops, owners would add a few things in my grocery for free. Even when I wore my cross around my neck, it didn't faze them. I was told that 'we look after our kind'. I always thanked them ever so much, as at the end of the day, really people are all the same.

My relationship with Brad was getting even worse. I eventually stopped doing cocaine, as it had got to a point that I almost thought I was going to die. I was consuming from one to three grams a day; it all came to me for free. I had been sitting on the floor one day and my heart was racing and then my nose was bleeding. Brad took it so casually and got me to drink orange juice. I promised that was the last day I would touch the stuff; I believed I was losing my mind and health and Brad was evil – that he was getting me dependant on him. I was determined not to lose sight of the real me.

Brad was working as a council worker during the day and never came home until 3 am – if he came home at all. When he did, he smelt of perfume and was so high that I had to put him in bed. When I questioned him, he would yell at me and grab me around my throat and slam me against the wall and tell me how I was no good. There were nights when I had to sleep in the garage on a thin mattress, as he was violent and I could not go to my parents' place. I didn't want anyone getting involved with the drama I was in. I had got myself into this mess; I had to get myself out. It was a low time in my life and I asked myself: being so smart, how did I allow this to happen? Easy: he got at my weakness and knew how to mess with my mind.

My neighbour used to get me to come over and stay there with me for hours, as it was the one place where Brad could not enter. She used to hear him yelling at me in the unit. She spoke to me and motivated me to put a plan together to get out of there. She used to tell me that things would get better. I could not see that at the present moment.

Even when I was at my darkest time, I always managed to help friends. One of my old workmates needed a few months of staying somewhere, as she was having problems with her mother. I knew how she was feeling and took her in; I didn't even ask Brad, I just took her in. Eva and I helped each other at our lowest times. Brad lost his cool a few times in front of Eva and she could see how bad the relationship was. There were times I would make dinner and Brad would throw the food on the wall with the plate. He used to do that quite a bit, and then I stopped cooking altogether.

My Australian grandad passed away and left me an inheritance of vintage coins dating back from the 1880s; I loved collecting coins and stamps. One day, I went to check for them where I had hidden them in the garage and they had vanished. I was so upset – I was not worried about the value of the items, but it came from my adopted grandad, the man who helped my family out with all matters when my parents had first settled in Guilford. I knew that Brad had taken them, and I confronted him. I was even more sickened to find out that he had sold the collection. He just laughed. I never forgave him, and it just made me more determined to try and get out of the position I was in.

I would spend my time on the balcony watching the ocean and at times I would feel so lucky to see whales frolicking past me. I was grateful and appreciated those moment; even though I was in a bad situation, I still was grateful. Slowly, I was gaining strength with the thought of leaving Brad; it was a plan in the making.

But as soon as I thought that things were looking good for me, I found out that I was six weeks pregnant. I was so upset that I was pregnant again – how could I have this baby to a monster? Even if I left Brad, he would be tied to me and the baby forever. He was dangerous, and I was living a dangerous life.

I was torn between religion, culture and my past. I wanted to keep the baby, but my mind was telling me otherwise. I fell into depression, which I managed to cover up from my family and friends very well. I wanted to keep the pregnancy, so when I had enough courage, I told Brad. He went into a fit and got violent and started throwing things around. I was worried that he was going to strike me, so I left and spent an hour or so walking around the coastline. I took myself to the lighthouse at Vaucluse and sat there. I asked myself again how I had gotten into a position with a dangerous man who was trying to isolate me from my family and friends. When my sister came over I found out that Brad even had me followed. He had two guys following us, to make sure that we were kept in line and were not talking to the opposite sex. My sister knew what position I was in and I didn't want harm coming to my family. I knew I needed a plan of escape; it was just figuring out how I could do it. My sister was very supportive with what I told her about the pregnancy. She was more worried about my safety. I thought about all this while sitting down and watching the ocean. I walked back, and Brad had calmed down about the pregnancy. He said that he would make the booking to abort it, as he was not having another child. He never asked me how I was feeling and what I wanted.

The day came when I was taken to the Surry Hills clinic. Flashes of my first abortion came back to me and my emotions got the better of me. Tears streamed down my face. Brad looked at me, and I stopped in my tracks.

'Wipe your face. You're going through with this, got it?'

He grabbed my arm very firmly and pulled me towards the clinic. I was numb. It was over like that, and the clinic gave me a contact to see in North Shore. I took their advice, as one of the nurses had asked me a few questions. I was not embarrassed that I needed to speak to someone. It was the last straw; I felt my bubble was going to burst.

Two weeks later, I went to see a counsellor; she looked at me and said that I was very strong and that I 'needed to leave the pig'. I will never forget those words! It turned out that what I had needed was a stranger to tell me that I was strong. I could see then that there was a light at the end of the tunnel for me, and that it seemed like no matter what challenge came my way, I would climb that mountain and would eventually conquer it. I only saw the counsellor twice, but it was enough to get me going with a plan to leave Brad.

I applied to commercial agencies, as I could not work full-time, and I needed something to get my mind thinking on a positive path. I started getting a few roles, like as an extra for *Superman Returns*. A few friends of mine including Eva were on set all weekend; it was great to have that. I did a commercial for Holden and played a few roles in the background for some Australian dramas. I actually enjoyed doing that, though I needed to get back into getting a regular income. I applied for a job at Zet Zippers in Marrickville as a sales representative selling zippers and other must-need items for the fashion industry. I got the job and was the only Australian working in the company of Chinese employees who hardly spoke English. This was great, as it was a way of getting into the fashion industry again and being a rep. on the road was challenging but rewarding. It was also going to open the pathway for my future business: Oxi Clothing.

I also managed to get my fitness back up by attending Bondi Gym. Brad hated the idea of me going there on my own and decided that he would come and be my minder. He could see the change that was coming over me and he knew now that the hold he had on me was not scaring me anymore.

My girlfriends from the clothing store in Parramatta, Eva (who had moved out by then) and Monique, were always there for me. I was so thankful at that time of my life to have them close to me. If it wasn't for them, I don't know how I would have gotten through that chapter of my life.

The plan came into place: I had to get out. Monique knew what was going on, and while Brad was at work, we managed to get a removalist and move all my things into storage. Monique wanted me to stay with her and her husband in their place until I found a place to live, and although I was hesitant at first, I did accept the offer and moved in with them, in the eastern suburbs. I had no intentions of moving back to my unit in Merrylands, as this would have been a backward step for me after what had happened to me in that unit. I had already made up my mind that I was going to sell it when I thought the market was right.

My mother begged me to come back and live with them, but I didn't want to as it would have been a risk with my father, and because I didn't want Brad going there knocking on the door. Being with Monique and her husband was a safe haven for me. Just like that, I moved out, leaving the key on the floor for him. The only thing he had was his bed – the rest was history.

'I'm thankful for my struggle because without it I wouldn't have stumbled across my strength.'

— ALEX ELLE

My Fighter

Becoming a Boxing Coach: New Path

'You've only got three choices in life:
Give up, Give in, or
Give it all you've got.'

— Unknown

Eva approached me one day in October 2005 and mentioned that her boyfriend was an amateur boxer at the world famous Kostya Tszyu boxing academy, and the man himself, a four-time light welterweight world champion – having also spent a period of time as the undisputed champion of that division – was looking for a female boxing coach. He wanted to start off with classes for beginners and teach the basic drills and how to throw punches.

I accepted the offer, and the meeting was set up to meet him and Igor, his brother-in-law, the following Monday at 6 pm. I have always been a person who had two jobs: one full-time and stressful, and the other would be fitness. I started to doubt myself: I was wondering why a man of his status would want to meet me. What did I have to offer?

I had just moved into my Petersham apartment – it was weird; life had come back full circle for me. I was living less than a block from where my father started his humble beginnings on Wardell Street. I walked over there and gazed at the unit block that he had once lived in. I walked along Frazer Street and sat on the swing that my parents used to push me on. It felt good; I had made the right choice by leaving the struggles behind and in how I had dealt with each of them. I was strong, and I was not going to allow anyone to ever make me feel bad about myself again, or make me feel like I was worth nothing. That was the last straw. I was breaking the circle of being with men who treated women with no respect. No more being with the bad boy image type. I wanted to surround myself with men who cared and had a purpose in life – and the same with the friends I wanted around me.

I was now living closer to Zet Zippers in Marrickville and I was happy to be renting a small one-bedroom unit. It was very small, though I was happy; it was nothing flash, just basic. I ended up staying there for five years; it served its purpose until I was ready to move and sell my apartment in Merrylands.

Monday came, and after work I arrived at the PCYC Rockdale to this world-class academy. I stood at the bottom of the stairs, engulfed with nerves. *Silvana, please shake this feeling off: you're about to face the man himself.* I walked up the stairs, lined with my qualifications. When I entered the gym – boy, oh boy; I walked into the smell of shirtless, sweaty men training. I could see why a gym like this would deter women. I could also see where Kostya was taking this by hiring a female trainer. He wanted to cater for women getting into boxing and make this a place where boxing could be a fitness regime for women and men alike. What a great idea, to welcome more women in a male-dominated sport!

All eyes were on me. I walked through and was guided to Kostya's office. I was ready. I walked in, and there was his brother-in-law, Igor, sitting on the desk and Kostya leaning over the table. They introduced themselves and talked about what they wanted from a trainer. I gave my five-minute speech of what I could offer to the gym and its clients. Within half an hour, Kostya had made his decision.

'Silvana, you are a very strong woman and you are someone that can handle the personalities in here. Can you make it next Monday for the classes at 7 pm? I will be here and see how you perform under pressure with me watching you conduct the class.' He spoke in a strong Russian accent.

'Yes, Kostya, I'll see you next Monday.'

We shook hands and I was to make my mark next Monday for class. I walked out with the boxers in training looking at me and I felt a sense of achievement: it was a small victory. What was it that this ex-pro boxer saw in me? I was going to find out on Monday.

I called Eva and thanked her boyfriend Justin so much, as I was going to be given a chance of conducting a class on Monday. They were so excited for me. I had planned my class and went through everything that a regular person could do in a boxing class. I put together a plan where clients could do the same drills as a pro or amateur boxer: the class would cater for a regular client.

Monday night came, and I had eighteen people in my class, all males. Some kept going to Kostya, thinking that he and Igor was taking the class. When they asked who, they pointed at me. The looks I got from some were priceless, but others I could hear saying that this was a great idea: a female trainer in the gym was excellent. In 2005, I became the first female boxing coach at the Tszyu gym.

The class began right on 7 pm. Who would not be nervous having a former world champion watch your every move? I took the class for an hour. When it finished, a few guys came up and thanked me. Everybody was sweating, and even the guys who thought they were fit had struggled with the class.

'Silvana,' Kostya said. He came up to me and put his hand on my shoulder. 'I'd like to offer you a casual position here; you did amazing. The guys like you. You can coach here on Mondays and Wednesdays.'

'Kostya, what is it that you see in me, to want me stay on?' I needed to know. 'I feel honoured that I am working here now.'

'You're tough and you are a hard-working person.'

He left me with a sense of strength. My life flashed before me; I had gone on a massive journey, one that many people would have not survived, and the man himself saw that in my eyes.

Wednesday came, and that evening I had the same numbers, which was great – I had not scared off anyone. Kostya sat in again and watched me take class. He smiled at me. I knew in my heart that he had made the right choice. I was going to be the mentor, coach, friend and the inspiration for others to excel. I wanted people to feel good about themselves when they came to train – and that did happen.

I stayed at the academy for ten years, teaching class on Monday and Wednesday nights. This part of my journey shaped me to excel both in my full-time jobs and in my private life. I didn't have to be well off. It was the knowledge that I had that empowered myself to take control of my life and not to be a victim of my past, regardless of what had happened to me. I had the courage to speak up and say no to things and give my opinion without being too dominant. I conquered a lot during my time as a boxing coach – and still do today. I had my times of blood, sweat and tears, and standing up for what I believed in. I gained my respect by standing my ground as a woman in boxing. It is safe to be powerful – in any industry – as long you know how to be powerful in a loving way that benefits others as well as yourself. Teaching boxing helped me get over health issues and excel in my jobs; I grew up emotionally and mentally.

Kostya and Igor always helped me out with what I should add into my classes until I mastered the whole drill of boxing. I remember that one night, Kostya had come to me after class and asked if I could tone down the class, as I had people vomiting. I reminded Kostya that this was a boxing class, not the boxing-fit classes that were coming up now. Clients had a real class, though I took on his advice without a thought and toned the class down.

I faced many challenges teaching classes and keeping them exciting. It was only after a year that women clients got wind that I was teaching. I never really advertised at first, it was all word of mouth. I would always have trainers from other gyms come to see how my classes were conducted. I even got a trainer from the NRL football club who would come and do the class; I would always spot them. Boxing taught me to read people straight away. I could read someone's body language and what their next moves were going to be. I knew these people went back and took some points for their training session; I was honoured that they got word of my training style.

I always watched how other boxers moved in the ring, and I was never afraid to ask about something. I was not only a coach: I believe you are always learning. I observed other trainers that came to the gym to train for fights and watched their styles. I also worked with Kostya's friend, John, in the ring. He would always get me in the ring for sparring, and I even got a chance to spar with a taekwondo Olympian who was working on her skills for boxing, aware that boxing was not yet legal in the Olympic games just yet. I was a bit hesitant at first, as she was young and quick on her feet, and there was me: twice her age. Then there was also the Russian athlete who I would get in the ring and spar with when she was in Sydney. That also helped bring my skills up, as she showed me how to throw punches. I am always happy to take things on board and learn and build on that.

In 2012, I managed to put a training programme together of one-and-a-half hours on Saturdays, running for four weeks, with boot camp boxing. This went really well. I ran these programmes during the autumn and beginning of spring. I ran them for just over two years and at the time they went really well. There were a lot of drills of both outdoors and indoors, combining the workouts of amateur boxing.

The PCYC fitness centre started a programme to get youths who were in trouble with the law to do my class, without other clients knowing who they were. There was always a member of the police present while the classes were conducted. I often got asked by clients doing the class why I had a police officer sitting and observing the class. I was always truthful and told them the reason for the police being there. Everybody was understanding and thought what the PCYC was doing was a great idea.

A few times, I had some of the boys challenge my authority and laugh at me, because I was a female coach and what did I know about boxing? I would go straight up to them and look at them straight in the eye and tell them, very firmly, that if they didn't like the class they could get out. I knew that at the end of the day, if they didn't finish the programme they would go to a correction centre. Police officers would never get involved, as there was no threat and I think they were happy that there was a female coach telling it how it was.

One night, I had one of these youths come up to me and thank me after he had finished his programme. He told me that I helped him through his darkest time and that he wanted to come back to my class and be a better person. He said that he had never come across a female boxing coach before and that he respected how I held myself and it was because of me that he saw life through a different set of eyes. I was so happy that I had given someone a wealth of knowledge. Using my authority in a way that helped others – it touched my heart, and he kept coming to my class and I watched him grow and develop. I was so happy, nothing else mattered to me. I watched him turn that page to change his life. He ended up moving to the next class and I watched him develop towards wanting to be a boxer. I had made a change in a small way, though the programme ended after a few years.

I became a part of the furniture at this boxing gym. The years passed, and I was able to grow and develop and at the same time watch many clients come through and train – some remain there today, and others come and go. But the women I taught to fight with the aim of competing in a boxing ring never made it into the ring. It is a hard journey, and boxing is a very lonely sport; you need real mental toughness to get through the training.

One thing I learnt was to read people within a minute. Being a trainer, you are able to read many people that walk through the door. I always say to my clients: never judge anyone, even if you decided to fight in the ring. I was able to read when someone was going through depression, and which women that came through were being physically abused. I picked up on the body language straight away and felt it was my duty to get the message across in a discreet way that I was there to listen. Not only was I a trainer, I was a mentor – though when you train fighters or clients in any fitness exercise, you become somewhat of a counsellor. Your duty is to help them get out of their darkness, to be able to overcome the fear that they have come across, and get them to climb that mountain and be able to see what is there for them waiting. When you have experienced life and gone through great challenges, you are much wiser and stronger and not ashamed to stand your ground. I was happy to be the sounding-board for many clients that came through the door. Even when I was going through my own challenges, I was there to listen.

I met my future husband through boxing and he would help me with the classes. He was able, like me, to pick the clients that were going through a very difficult time and he and I would chat after class and come up with a plan to help them through fitness, and get them through the challenges that had come their way.

From all that, there were plenty of times during the ten years I was working at the boxing gym that I had clients come to me after class and tell me that I had saved them from destruction, and that coming to my classes was an outlet. Some had gone through such terrible times and I was able to listen, because I had gone through my journey and I was able to relate to them. I made sure I catered for everyone in my classes. I was able to teach the beginners and the advanced and even though it was hard, I made sure that everyone was looked after and was challenged throughout their workouts.

My journey continued to grow, even though I had clashed over the years with some trainers that came through the gym because their attitude was that a female wouldn't know anything about boxing. I stood my ground and I never backed down. But on the other hand, there were also trainers and boxers who welcomed me with open arms and expected that there would be a female boxing coach.

It became easier when female boxing became legal for the Olympics in 2012. It took a long time to get to that equal opportunity.

I always get asked: 'Have you ever boxed?' and, 'How did you get into coaching?'

No, I have never fought, just sparred in the ring with other boxers. I could not fight back in the day, because it was not legal; the door opened up for me to become a boxing coach and I grabbed that opportunity with both hands, and made my mark in a small way.

I represented a few times in my husband's corner, where twice he won his division. I was there to help him with his diet and training. He was originally a kickboxer and had eight bouts in boxing at amateur level. I also had the opportunity to be a trial judge a few times with a lady called Jill, without whom I do not know how amateur boxing NSW, would go on today without her. It was she who encouraged me and told me firmly to stay in boxing as a coach, even when I was getting a hard time handling the attitude of some of the men in the industry. She encouraged me to stay; I almost left because of the comments that came my way, but she reminded me that she too had endured a similar fate back in her day.

I'm sure it would have been more difficult for her, than me. Jill paved the way for women and men in boxing. She had made her mark in a huge way and kept telling me that we needed more women like me to make that mark and open the doors for other women to enter the sport. These men knew nothing about me and what my journey had been to get to this point. I stayed due to her and my future husband. I reminded myself that the comments and the nasty attitudes that floated around were due to the insecurities of others and it was not my problem, it was theirs.

In 2013 I was given an opportunity to represent the Tszyu gym for a charity event that was to take place at the Ivy Ballroom, Sydney. Khalil, co-owner of Tszyu boxing gym, believed that I should be able, as a female coach, to represent the three fighters I had at the time. My husband, Ken, wanted to fight and had asked me and I accepted – I was really grateful. As you can imagine, it's not easy for women to represent men in their corner, as many think women do not know what they're talking about when it comes to boxing, or that they're not strong enough to hold pads for their fighters when training. Either way, the door opened. OK, I might not have known everything, but I was there to give it a go and give it my best shot. I trained everybody, using my free time and making sure everybody was pulling their weight. My poor husband helped me with the other fighters on top of his training and working full-time for both of us. We were fighting for a cause: the Camp Quality charity.

The night went really well: I ended up at the last-minute fighting against my boss, Igor, who was representing another fighter from our gym. Though my husband fought well, at forty-five years old, I was so proud of him. I had another fighter who didn't win, but it was the most talked-about fight of the night, as the skill had come out from both fighters in the way they moved around the ring. Even though Sam , who was one of my three fighters for the charity event, didn't win, he didn't fall: he held his ground and that was more important than anything. He was up against a very great fighter and I was happy – it was his first fight in front of a sold-out crowd.

The last fight was the main event in which I had my last fighter, who my husband helped me in the corner with. Just picture Goliath and David, David being my fighter, Carlos. I knew the other team, which was a big corporation that I was up against; they thought they had this in the bag. Like I mentioned before: never underestimate your opponent – this was the mistake they made. They saw a female coach in the corner and laughed. I held my poker face and spoke to Carlos. By the end of the second round, Carlos was feeling unsure and uneasy and I told him to land those punches to the ribs.

'He's too tall: you need to go for the ribs and land those points – forget the head. You are not going to win if you keep aiming at the head.'

Carlos looked at me and I knew he had taken on board what I had told him. He got up and was charged. He landed those punches to the body. When the fight was over, I stood there with Ken and waited for the judges to make their decision. Carlos' arm went up and the referee announced the winning corner was red. It was us: we had won. We got cheers, though obviously some people were not happy that we had won. But who cared? I did it – I showed myself and overcame the fear that I had. Of course I was just as good as any male coach, and I deserved like no other to be in the corner and represent male fighters.

The photo of Carlos and me hangs on the wall at my home: it was a picture-perfect moment of the trainer in the corner talking to her fighter. Every time I look at it, it reminds me anything is possible. I had a dream to represent fighters in the corner, and I did it.

It was great that I had experienced boxing from all sides: being a coach, a trainer and a trial judge with Jill. I was able to see what judges were looking for and from what angles and how to score points without going hard with a punch. I learnt so much from Jill and I am grateful she had those stern words of wisdom for me to never to have that disbelief in my abilities again. I also met a great couple, John and Anna, who were promoters – even today, they are well-respected in the boxing industry, and I worked at most of their boxing events, helping with the VIP tables and guests. I was able to see what it was like putting an event together. I ran into the wonderful couple in early 2016 when Anna was applying to be a boxing promoter. I was so happy when she told me that she was applying. I encourage women to go into industries that are male-dominated and make their mark. Who says that we cannot do it – and do it right?

In 2012, I had an associate who lived in Asia and wanted to make a documentary called *Iron Psyche* on women in boxing. At the time, I only knew men who fought; I asked one of the boys in the gym if he knew a good female fighter. He gave me a name, Shelly Watts, and I organised for this female fighter to be filmed at the boxing academy. The gentleman that was making this documentary filmed all day at the gym. I remember Ken and me getting there at 5am in the morning to make sure that the gym looked right for filming. I was happy for women's boxing to get the exposure it needed. Well, this lady made a name for herself a few years later and ended up winning the gold for Australia in the Commonwealth Games in boxing event for women. She put amateur boxing on the map for women; yet another woman had opened a door for more women to enter boxing. Boxing became legal for women to compete in the Olympics in 2012.

It has been a journey of blood sweat and tears. Boxing was not an easy sport to get into when I made my start, though I stayed, and I'll keep on, making my mark. Boxing has given me so much more; it has helped me with my private life, with my full-time jobs and being able to be an achiever in a given industry. It enabled me to stay focused and give me back my life. It helped me with health issues I had to overcome. I still took classes even when I was going through my biggest challenge - IVF. Boxing kept me going: the clients who kept coming, my husband who helped me with classes and other trainers who gave me advice with boxing drills – they all believed in me and gave me hope to never stop dreaming; anything is possible.

'Believe and achieve.'

Radio days

Designers flaunt it on the streets

They may not be the catwalks of Milan, but the streets of Newtown will host a weekend of fashion at Flaunt It, writes **Rashell Habib**.

Making the News

Going Into Business: The Making of Oxi Clothing

'Be so good that they cannot ignore you.'

— Steve Martin

I learnt a lot working at Zet Zippers for nine months. I was cold-calling fashion businesses in Sydney and Melbourne and building my network, who are now our leading fashion designers and companies. They all said the same thing: they all wanted exposure – to get their products out. I had an interest and was great at advising on how to market their products. I believed that at the time, Australia needed fashion designers to be recognised more. We had some amazing, talented designers but I felt I needed to move on from my job there. I was grateful that I had worked with a company with all Chinese employees as it helped me build my confidence in approaching businesses to talk about the products I was offering.

I put a plan together: I was going to open a clothing store in three months. Aside from working, I spent my days sourcing labels – not just any labels, I was looking for up-and-coming designers. I wanted to cater for both men and women. It was about being fresh and edgy, with a lot of sex appeal. This was going to be a destination store, where people would think, 'I need something different to wear, let's go there first'.

How funny, that my father wanted me to be a fashion designer by force and here I was, about to open my own clothing store. This had come full circle; it was my time to go into business, without being forced by my father or anyone else. I was still working as a boxing coach two nights a week – that never stopped, and if anything, it helped me to stay focused in business and to teach and train and to be a strong, centred businesswoman.

I scoped areas which would suit the demographic for Oxi Clothing. I came up with the name Oxi because it stood for 'oxygen fresh' and something new. I spent my nights off looking at the areas

I wanted the store in; I picked out Surry Hills, Cronulla, Newtown and Bondi Beach. I had a few questions first though that I would tick off the list: if people had expandable income in the area, who lived in the area and who it was that I wanted to target. I would also go into the other stores and see the labels that they carried; all stores were carrying the same labels in almost every store. I had an advantage – by working at Zet Zippers, especially in Melbourne, I had labels that no-one knew about. I had also been a mystery shopper to see how the customer service was and how the stores were laid out. I gathered my information and took that all on board.

It was a difficult time to be branching out with my own business, but even the racism couldn't stop me. The Cronulla riots broke out in December 2005 and racism was ripe. I constantly got asked 'are you Christian or Muslim?' I was sick of this – even wearing a cross around my neck, I was still getting asked. Even today I get asked, though I always throw it back at them (depending if it's work-related or social). I'm not afraid to speak up. Small, petty minds and people who have not been exposed to different cultures, are afraid of anything different.

But my brother got it worse. He was working as a driver delivering soft drinks for a major company. He was looking after the Cronulla area, and they had to take his run off him and put him out West, as he had rocks thrown at the truck by school kids in the playground. He had an Iranian worker with him, and I remember him telling me how his customers didn't want him in the shop anymore, until this blew over. The customers he had laughs with that smiled when he walked in, were all in a different frame of mind now. My heart was broken; I was so angry hearing this. They ended up putting a fair guy with blond hair on the run. Soon after, my brother sold his truck, and just like that decided to make a change and packed up and moved to Perth.

People do not understand that a word or an action, can have such an implication on people, whether it's good or bad. We just have to remember that it's the minority that do this. When people do not have a clear understanding about things or have insecurities, it shows – and sometimes violence and disputes happen, because of this.

We as Australians are lucky that we live in a country that gives its people great support, when other countries do not even have a public health system. Some of us that live in this great country complain about our everyday lives, when we should be grateful and say thank you for giving me what I have today and every day.

'If you're not happy, make that change and stop blaming others for your unhappiness and your undoing.'

At the time, I had met and started dating a man who was a few years younger than me. Samuel was a carpenter, gifted at making things. I wanted a break from the type of men I had gone out with before and went out with someone who was the total opposite. He was all into fitness, mediation and boxing. Samuel mentioned that he would help me with putting the store together. I managed to get Monique and her husband to help me with getting the fixtures made, as he was in construction. My gay friend Antonio, who at the time sold wholesale jewellery, was my mentor for a while when it came to business decisions, with planning and financial matters. Antonio grabbed me one day and we walked into the Commonwealth Bank. Just like that, I took out a $30,000 loan to open the store. I am talking about everything had to be in that budget, including store fixtures, clothes, displays, mannequins and paying contractors.

I was a risk taker, as I was now renting in Petersham and paying off a mortgage. I had little money to fall back on, though I needed to do this and Antonio knew I could pull it off. Still, it was a stretch and I knew that.

I had John, who I sparred with at the boxing gym, help me source the leasing agreement and see the location. I was drawn to the southern end of King Street, Newtown, where there were only two stores: Drag Star Women's Clothing and Made, which catered for men and women's clothing, though it was nothing like the line I was bringing in. I was approached by a landlord, who had a new shop that was empty and needed a tenant. I negotiated the rent with him and saw the area – it was opposite the famous café that was the Chocolate Dog Café by day and by night it went Mexican, run by different owners. I was also next door to the Union Hotel and the bus stop was just in front of my store. I believed in the potential to take the store, which also had two car spaces downstairs. John advised me to take the store, which I did, and all he wanted from me was a box of beer in return. I was blessed to have such amazing people around me who wanted me to see my dream come to reality. I believe that by hanging around people who are driven and positive in life, it only takes you upwards.

I signed the lease agreement and took the store. Eva and Monique with Samuel and Antonio kept very close in my circle and would help me in so many ways. Eva and Monique were in the modelling and commercial industry, so I used them as the face of Oxi Clothing. These girls also helped with two of the fashion parades that Oxi Clothing was in. I began with transforming the store into a place where people could come in, shop and relax. I bought a red couch, which funnily enough became a counselling couch for people to come and chat to me when I was not busy.

With $30,000, I opened my store. Some of the business owners in the area were amazed how I opened the store on that amount. I had to buy all my stock up front, as I had no history with the suppliers and no-one knew who I was. That all changed in three months, as I have always been told that suppliers must be paid first: you must always keep a great relationship with them, as it's a small industry and word gets around fast, so keep the suppliers happy. I did a course that the government was offering at the time, about opening a small business and how to keep it going – it was free, and was such a great programme to be in. I managed to make the time to network in my community of Newtown and go to business information nights that benefited Oxi Clothing. I always wanted to be informed and network with people; I wanted to be the face now, as the businesswoman of Oxi Clothing. I wanted people to take me seriously and wanted them to see that a woman could do it. I had no financial backing, though it was something I needed to tick off my bucket list; I wanted to see if I had it in me to open a business on my own.

Do not get me wrong, it was hard work transitioning from getting a fortnightly income, to getting paid when you can. I had a lot of people tell me that I opened in the wrong place and that the store would never survive. These are the people that had no goals and had no inspiration to excel and do something. They were afraid of their own shadow.

In April 2006, the store opened. Kostya and Igor attended the opening and I was surrounded by family, friends and a DJ named Murat who was just starting to get recognised, soon to explode in the club scene. He would DJ a few times for me at fashion events and I would get him on Saturdays to DJ in the store window, where I pulled in the shoppers – a great way to market. It was such a great night. I had done it: I opened the store and now was all about keeping it going. They say most businesses fail within a year and I was determined to fight and had the passion to bring something fresh into Newtown.

I had come a long way, with boxing helping me get focused and having the right people around me. I crossed the road and looked at my store. I had come through very challenging life events and I knew there and then that I was one tough woman. I looked above and thanked God and my angels that had looked after me and put me back on my path – this fighting spirt had come back with a vengeance!

Within a fortnight, Oxi Clothing was in the local paper for being the fresh new kid on the block and bringing in up-and-coming Australian designers. From there, I would get the shop out by doing letterbox drops after work in the local area, and also networking with the local businesses in the area. I also recognised a strong gay community in the area and decided to put my rainbow triangle sticker in the window to let the clients know I supported them. Soon after that Oxi Clothing had the gay community coming in and supporting the store. For me to have that, I had been accepted in the community and also realised my product was different and fresh and people wanted me to keep bringing more.

I was invited to social events, business events and fashion parades. Suppliers and designers wanted me to carry their clothing lines. When I first opened, I had to actually put in a submission for the reason why I wanted a label in the store. The store was judged on location and how it was presented. A lot of consumers do not know that to carry a clothing line, the designer or supplier looks at the store first before their product is represented there.

Oxi Clothing was moving forward fast. I worked hard six to seven days a week, working on the buying before the store opened and then working in the store. It got to a point that I was burning out, so when my sister came back from England, she helped me on some Sundays. I eventually had three staff that helped me on the weekends, though I could not have them working all at once. What I did was to bring in a staff member on the hours where we needed that second person to cover for the rush, and I would put someone on to run the store by themselves when I felt they were confident enough. I worked every second Sunday, as I had to keep costs down. The weekends were our money-making days. I had to make sure that everyone knew the products and knew how to give excellent customer service and sell.

The store was getting recognised for the funky displays that were always themed in the window. I had people from TV stations, people coming from Cronulla and Manly, even NRL players at the time, buying the most amazing t-shirts that I was sourcing from Melbourne and Perth, with the occasional Sydney brands.

I had to stay on top of the game, as we had store owners coming in from other boutiques wanting to know what the fuss was about and picking up on the brands. My friends and clients always kept me informed about other stores that started carrying the labels I had, so I would change labels. I needed to keep it vibrant and needed to stay afloat. This was my bread and butter: I had no financial support, I was living week-to-week, and most times I was living off a can of tuna and rice crackers, or brown rice. I wanted to get the store to a level where I knew I could pull this off, despite all the bills, mortgage and rent. I had to make this work: if it was working then I was doing something right. I had a business plan, and I always went back to that when I started to feel a bit overwhelmed.

In 2007, I decided to give Oxi Clothing more exposure by using social media. I put it on Facebook and created a website that I had to update myself. I even decided to create online shopping, though this was ahead of its time for retail and it did not work out.

I advertised a few times in the *Sydney Observer* and soon enough I was getting recognised even more. Oxi Clothing was in the local paper a few times and also the Glebe paper. I had supported the local schools in the area, so the mums were coming in, wanting something different and new. My store was also was next door to a dominatrix who looked like Marilyn Monroe; she was a vixen, and people in the area loved her. I actually went into her townhouse one day and saw the world she lived in, with different themed rooms for her clients that came through. She explained that she had tradies, lawyers, couples and even actors that came to see her. I knew, as some of these people also came and bought from my store. I thanked her for giving me exposure.

I never judge, and I think this proved to be the biggest element of putting Oxi Clothing on the map. I had so many people from different walks of life walk in and buy. I always got asked how I was keeping the shop afloat when there was no foot-traffic on the south end and with the competition around. My response was that it was my customer service (I treated everyone like they were special), the clothing lines I carried in store, and that I always worked on window displays that people talked about. I never forgot that Stash Clothing had made that impact on me and I modelled the store and myself on that. Dianne knew what I had done, and she was so proud of me. I had learnt from the best businesswoman.

Well things started to pay off, as Oxi Clothing was a finalist four years in a row for the Inner Business Award. One day, I received a package from the Retail Association of NSW, saying that the store was nominated as a finalist for the NSW small boutique for outstanding achievement and store presence. I accepted the invite, though I had to put in a submission of why my store was succeeding and a little write-up on the store. I followed the procedure and before you knew it, I was taking Monique to this black-tie event at Pyrmont's Doltone house. We got there, with women all in cocktail dresses and men in black ties and suits. We took our seats, sitting amongst Mitre Ten and Gloria Jeans who were some of the other retailers that were in the finals.

Monique was so surprised. 'Silvana, you are amongst the most recognised retailers in this country! You should be so proud of yourself.'

I was in disbelief that a little store like Oxi Clothing was sitting amongst big retailers like Best&Less and Sussan. I had been recognised and voted as one of the most outstanding retailers in NSW. I had proved to myself that I was a great operator; I now classified myself a businesswoman who brought an unknown shop to the community on the map. Even though I did not win, I was a finalist for NSW small boutique and that meant a lot to me – more than anything.

I thanked Monique for her constant support and her belief in me. I looked at her and remembered how a few weeks after Oxi Clothing opened, she had come up and presented me with photos of me winning the Ms Fitness and Ms East Coast Australia. She had these blown up and framed, and together we put both on the wall next to the register. Monique showed me that I should be proud and always to look at those photos and to remind me of how far I had come, and that I should not be ashamed of my achievements. My trophies and photos had been packed away before then, because Brad, my ex-boyfriend, had never wanted them around. I was happy that Monique graced me with her present and I was happy that I had chosen her to accompany me to the awards that night.

My boyfriend Samuel also helped me in so many ways; he would play such an important role in my life. He softened me when my walls were up; he showed me more than ever that I could be powerful in a loving way. We would go together to meditate twice a week and it would help me, as I am the type of person who is always constantly on the go. He would always buy me books of self-empowerment and meditation so that I could balance my energy.

Oxi Clothing was selected by the city of Sydney and Marrickville council as one of the most fashion-forward stores in the area. A fashion parade was going to be held at the Marlborough Hotel on King Street, Newtown. It was a big event; the council decided to give more exposure for the stores that were quirky and different. It was free of charge for the shops involved, and advertising and the set-up of stages and venue was looked after by the council. The only thing I did was to find eleven models, of all different sizes and backgrounds. The event was voluntary, but I paid for their time in clothing – it was only fair. I had friends who also wanted to help with make-up and hair – and the make-up, which was applied to all sexes, was amazing.

It was a great event; the upstairs bar at the Marlborough was so full that the security guards had to turn people away. One of the models, Vaska, who was only twenty-one at the time, had blown the crowd away with her beauty. Vaska was someone who turned heads in a crowded room, and she was wearing lingerie and a lace jacket with a fake fur collar that only had one button done up at the waist, and black heels. When I dressed her I wanted to make a statement, that there was nothing wrong with women feeling sexy and claiming their beauty and being proud. Well it worked: the Oxi Clothing fashion parade was applauded with its fashion-forward looks for both guys and women. I had some of the male models take off their tops on the edge of the catwalk and it got all the females screaming. I wanted the store to stand out from the rest.

The store was a hit, and within a week Oxi Clothing had a write-up in the local paper, sales tripled for a month after the parade, and Oxi Clothing was selected again for a private, expenses paid, fashion show at a college in Camperdown. So for a few weeks, the vibe in Newtown was high, as the parade went really well. But I was having issues with Samuel: even though he was great, he had his own battles to deal with – self-confidence issues of not thinking he was good enough. He felt that he was never on my level, so I encouraged him to see a counsellor. I went with him, as I believed that you needed to work on the relationship and not just give up.

One day he came to my work, saying that he was going to Qatar for six months tomorrow for work. I looked at him.

'Samuel, you never told me you were going! I am in shock. Tomorrow? I am only finding out about this now.'

'Yes, I told you plenty of times.'

'OK, I am not going to argue with you about leaving; this is not the first time you've packed up and let me know that you're going for work somewhere with less than twenty-four hours' notice – or no notice at all.'

Samuel worked as a carpenter on the set of some major movies. I was grateful that I got to go to the after party of *Wolverine*, which was held at the Piano Bar, and also I got to go to the after party of the movie *Australia*, which was held at a secret location, and yes: I was graced by the presence of the major actors, like Hugh Jackman and Nicole Kidman, who were in those movies.

Like that, Samuel was gone to work on another project in Qatar. I could not stop him: he needed to sort out whatever he was going through. It broke my heart that our relationship was like a light bulb for him: to be switched on when you wanted it and switched off when you didn't.

I threw myself into work and a wonderful woman came into my life and opened my eyes. She helped me make the decision to close my beloved store, Oxi Clothing. Online shopping was becoming a big thing now and frontline shops were being so affected that many shut their doors. Some major stores were running at a loss. It was a decision made by heart and mind together, and a weight that I had been carrying was lifted. What was it that I wanted in my life, and was I too scared to recognise it before it was too late?

In early 2010, I closed the store. My decision shocked everyone in the area and even today I thank my guardian angel Vaska for helping me make a choice that needed to be done.

'Life is short.
If there was ever a moment to follow your passion and do something
That matters to you,
That moment is now.'

— UNKNOWN

Vaska

Vaska, Ambassador of Angels

'Faith is not just believing in words.'

— Vaska Trajkovska

In early 2007, my sister – who had been living abroad in London for a few years with her girlfriends – called me and asked if I could hang out with a lovely woman who was coming back from living overseas. I was working at Oxi Clothing and assured her that I would have her under my wing. Vaska was going to be living back at her parents' place in St Peters. It was going to be a difficult transition from being abroad for so long and coming back to Sydney and living with her parents. I agreed to contact her and make arrangements to have her hang out with me. Even though there were thirteen years difference in age, it didn't bother me, as I was always young at heart and seemed to have younger friends gravitate to me.

So one day, this beautiful woman walked into the store and I knew for some reason that it was Vaska. She was striking: 5'7" with the perfect hourglass shape and wavy hair that sat perfectly on her body. She had looks I have not seen in a very long time and I knew she could model easily.

For some strange reason, I felt connected to this stranger – like I had known her for a very long time, though that didn't make sense. She introduced herself with the pearliest white smile and we hit it off, just like that. Vaska and I started hanging out; at first it was just here and there, then it was always. We would see each other after work and training – she even came to my boxing classes, which the boys loved, as she was a breath of fresh air. I would go over and hang out with her on the weekends. I also spent time showing her the town – our favourite place was Sunday nights at Hugo Lounge in Kings Cross. We even shared the same friends.

One night, we were out with friends from Brisbane and my sister who had come back to Sydney. We were all having a great night and of course Vaska's presence softened the hardest hearts. She had this glamour that was defined in every sense. I was wearing a short skirt and a long top which showed off how toned my legs were, as I was still into working out with weights. I was sitting there, minding my own business, and out of the blue this girl pointed at me and was laughing and kept pointing. I looked at her and looked around, as to make sure it was me she was referring to. Then a few people came in on her group and were looking at me. I saw her mouth call out 'tranny' at me. I walked over to her and, with a very firm tone over the music, I was in her face.

'Are you calling me a tranny? Are you calling me a tranny?'

She looked at me very horrified, seeing that I was a normal looking woman who happened to be fit. Her boyfriend jumped in to apologise and before you knew it, my sister and the girls in my group jumped in. She knew she had put a foot in it, and my sister, God bless, kept saying to her, 'you're dealing with the wrong person'.

It got out of hand; there were words being thrown around and security had to come and try to hold my sister and a few of my friends back. I began to think that punches were going to be thrown and I really didn't want to be throwing a punch, because I knew this girl would go down. This went on for ten minutes, then I was happy to go and told security that we would leave. I went up to this girl and whispered in her ear,

'Never judge a book by a cover. You should work on your insecurities and do something about getting into shape. I am twice your age and I still pick up guys your age. By the way, I am a boxing coach, so it's your lucky night, girlfriend.'

I walked away, grabbing my sister who was still calling out. It was getting late and we left to go home. Vaska sat in the back of the car with me and said that I handled myself really well; the situation could have been really bad. I looked at her and a tear came down my face.

'Vaska, you do not understand: it's not the first time I've been called a tranny. Why? Because I look strong, so I am a tranny?'

She grabbed my hand and looked at me, 'Sil, I have always been called a tranny because of my height. Women can get so insecure around other women, whether it is beauty or brains. You should never be ashamed of how you look. I admire your look.'

I had to remind myself that it was just words and that there are so many people in this world who are just not socially educated and do not know how to act in public. Vaska had put me at ease, knowing that someone like her had the same thing said to her in the past.

I had taken Vaska around a lot; we would drive down the coast and I remember one day we were parked next to a fire engine with a few firefighters inside. We all stood around, watching the people hang-gliding in the air. We managed to strike up a conversation and chat for a while. It was a moment that I cannot describe, it was like Vaska was unconsciously aware that her time with us would be brief – like me, she followed her heart and truly lived in the moment. I saw myself in her and realised that I had forgotten for a while to live. I had the store, and it made me feel caged, like my life was passing by while I sat in the store day in and day out, burning the candle at both ends. My life with Samuel was going nowhere and I felt my heart was calling out for something else, something more meaningful. I watched in awe as she chatted, so childlike, giggling and every man there was in a spell. She looked over at me and said, 'Silvana, we are doing hang-gliding next week. I am paying for this, it's your birthday and you never mentioned it to me.'

So the following week, we went hang-gliding at Stanwell Tops. I was at peace gliding through the air. I was given a gift and it made Vaska happy watching me fly through the sky. That same day, we went to Newton to watch my DJ friend perform at the park in St Peters. It was such a great event: we danced and laughed and just lived in the moment, and it brought me back to the days of Las Vegas. We were walking back to the store to get my car and Vaska insisted that I get a Siamese fighting fish as the aquarium was right there, staring me in the face, and because Vaska had them at home.

'Why do you want me to have a fighting fish Vaska?'

''Cause you're a fighter and the fish is a reminder that you can do it, and you can lead your own path. Because you cannot have a lion, can you now?' We both laughed, and I agreed to get one.

Even to this day, I always keep a fighting fish in my home, to remind me of my strength, determination and courage, and the path I have led. It's also to remind me of the beautiful relationship I had with Vaska. There was no age or time; we were close in a very short time. Maybe she was my angel and wanted to show me and teach me an important lesson in my life, because she came into my life so quickly and then like that, she was taken away from her friends and family.

I introduced her to Arq, a popular nightclub in Sydney, on Sundays and for a while it was great. We had our Sunday sessions there and then, just like that, we would flip and go to church in the city with Emma because we felt we were partying too much.

Vaska would come and look after my shop while I went to do the buying. At times, she would come and sit on my couch and eat her chicken cashew and talk to me about what I wanted in life and Samuel. Samuel was living with me, though he was in and out of my life as he pleased. He never wanted marriage and children, and Vaska reminded me what it was what I wanted in life. She said I had to do what was best for me and that I always put myself second best when it came to being in a relationship. If I wanted children, I had to put me first: I was getting close to forty years old. Samuel was a great guy, but I was outgrowing him and my journey was heading in a different direction to his. He came into my life and opened a closed flower and made me blossom. Samuel showed me what I truly wanted in a relationship.

For a while, Vaska travelled again through Europe, Thailand and India, which was one of her favourite places. She was drawn to helping others that were not so lucky, and her desire was to be involved in charity with helping orphaned children. She was always there for her friends and her family.

One day, she walked in to look after my shop and it was like this angel walked in: she was in a white top and blue jeans. I had gone with a friend to see a fashion parade and came back and wanted to take her across the road to have some Mexican food. She loved the place and the food and I wanted to do something for her, as she never took money from me for looking after the store.

We sat and talked, and it was such a weird feeling – it felt like it was the last supper with her. Vaska was talking to me like she was going somewhere. She looked at me, filled with inner peace, and said words that I will never forget and handed me two little pocketbooks. One was on the art of being calm and the other was on the Dalai Lama, which I have with me to this day.

'You promise me that you will do something about the store and Samuel. Listen to your heart and mind and act on it.'

I took everything she said on board and the night ended with me wondering: had I met a living angel that was trying to protect me and put me on the path that would mean I would eventually meet my future husband?

A few days passed; I remember it so clearly. I was working that Wednesday and I got a phone call. My sister was crying and saying that Vaska is gone, and she just kept repeating it. I closed the store and called Samuel, asking him to take me to Liverpool Hospital to see Vaska. I got there with her two older sisters, Vicky and Suzie, and her mother was sitting there too. Vaska looked so peaceful lying there. They allowed me and Samuel in, as we had become like family to them, and I realised that Vaska's lips were blue. I walked up to her and touched her hair.

Vaska had passed away that morning, at the age of twenty-one, on 7 May 2008. She died in her sleep, at a friends' place in Liverpool. She had four blood clots to her lungs. She had always told me that she would be young when she passed away; that she wanted to die in her sleep, at peace. For the moment, I looked at her and held her. I remembered when I was in hospital at a similar age with a blood clot that almost took my life away. I cried, my tears falling down her face. She was an angel who lived a short time on Earth and had made such an impact on the people she met.

I was asked to go to the morgue. I sat there for a while, stroking Vaska's hair and spoke to her like she was asleep. I knew what I had to do, and it was the thing she asked me to do before she passed away. Her funeral was held a few days later in Rockdale and she had people come from as far away as India to pay their respects. She was everybody's angel, and I am sure she touched everyone she spent time with very deeply, like she did with me.

I promised that I would remain in close contact with her sisters, which I still do today.

I managed to raise $3000 for the August 2008 city-to-surf charity run, which I donated to an orphanage. Vicky decided that she would take part with me. We did the charity run and, believe it or not, when we crossed the finish line, a picture of a present popped up on Vicky's phone, as an SMS with no number. It was really weird, and we both put it down as Vaska giving us the thumbs up.

Samuel, who had spent time with Vaska's little brother, ended up getting him to do karate in Alexandria. After what happened, he needed to do something that would be good for him. Vaska's passing really disturbed Samuel too.

A few years later, a very close friend of Vaska's who was living between India and London created the charity that Vaska had always wanted. Although her life was cut short, her dream was lived and the charity was created in her honour, to help the orphaned children in India.

Vaska 'Ambassador of Angels' was set up in June 2013.

'Vaska, you are a spirit, flames of fire, you have a greater connection even now with your loved ones today.'

Unplanned Chapter of My Life: The Unknown

'When you focus on the problems you will have more problems;
When you focus on possibilities you will have more opportunities.'

— Zig Ziglar

So I closed Oxi Clothing and sold my unit in Merrylands. As I was driving home one day, I stopped over at the park my parents had taken me to back when I was young. Something came over me as I watched the park, with people sitting down, getting some sunshine, and children with parents playing on the swings. I thought about Vaska and how Samuel had left me again on Christmas Eve in 2008. I had come home and seen a set of keys on the table. I knew he had gone and never told me. I looked in the wardrobe to find only a suit he had in there. I just could not do this anymore. I called him to see where he was, he said it was not my business and that he was in Queensland. I heard Vaska saying those words: *What are you going to do?* All that haunted me, with him switching this relationship on and off.

I drove home and waited for Samuel. I just sat there and before I knew it, the door opened. I must have sat there for a few hours. He looked at me and he knew it was over. I told him that I needed more in my life and that he was right: we were on different pages. I didn't want to waste my life anymore, hoping things would come to me. I had to go out and find it myself. I ended the relationship. I felt good because it was the best thing for Samuel and me. We kept in touch for a year after that, and then I never heard from him again. I was grateful to him for opening me, like I said before, to become a blossoming flower. He showed me a path of spiritual growth within that I thought I didn't have. I believe so much that you do meet people for a reason, whether it's for a short period or long, and there is a lesson we must learn from them.

I continued on an unplanned path; I worked with a few companies in clothing retail, either as a manager or area manager. I hated the way staff were being treated by top management. I had come from working on my own and now I was being micromanaged to do things. Half of the companies I worked for had a backward plan of how to run a company and it made me so frustrated that I changed jobs a few times. I was trying to find my path again, and then one day I was headhunted at East Gardens by a major clothing company. At first, I was really not sure, though I had an interview set up for me. I met with the state manager who went through my CV. He was impressed with what I had to offer and gave me the position of looking after six stores in the eastern suburbs, north shore, northern beaches and one at Miranda. I worked hard and it was not an easy job; I had about forty staff that I coached and also did the hiring and firing and all the rostering.

The long hours in retail were burning me out. My days off were not days off at all and it started to affect my private life. Some weeks I was doing sixty hours or more. I became a regional manager and didn't like how the regionals were being treated – crash and burn, which saw a lot of managers leave.

I continued to go out and socialise, trying to pass my time by joining a few dating sites. Eventually, going out on dates and meeting with men that just didn't do it for me became a story in itself. Maybe because I had experienced so much so really nothing grabbed my attention. It's funny: I would go out on some dates and the guy would look nothing like his profile picture. I would always be upfront and tell them and then I would walk away. I was not going to waste my time sitting there with someone who lied on their profile.

Then there are those guys that went on about what they had, what they wanted in a woman and what they did for work. They're the types who would try to make you feel insecure about yourself, so that you thought you had to go out with them. I always sat there and listened, then the conversation would turn to me. I would say something like, 'Yeah, I run six stores, train, teach boxing, have lived aboard' and so on. So many times I would say that then not hear from the guy again. I knew why: it was because they felt threatened to come up against a woman who had experienced life. Half these guys didn't have the balls to do half the things I had done, and especially when it came to boxing, they were gone.

It didn't bother me, as I had nothing to lose. I wanted a man that accepted me as a boxing coach, who loved the outdoors and who could cook – as I didn't. I worked two jobs and life for me was always on the go. I wanted a man that would accept a strong, independent woman, who was not insecure with having male friends around her and who worked in a male-dominated industry; someone who would accept his woman going out with friends and vice versa; a man that was secure within himself and would allow his woman to spread her wings and would support her in every idea or goal she went after. I was going to find that man.

I kept going out and dating – sometimes I would be dating up to four guys at a time. Why not? Men do it, and I always made it clear that I was in the dating scene. Some were fine about it; others were not. I was a straight-shooter and a few times I was told that I was like a bloke on the dating scene because I dated more than one guy and never chased after them with text messages and phone calls. I believe that if a man wants you then no matter what, he will make an effort to see you and keep in contact with you. After what I had been through, I was not going to take the mind games of dating; if you want to know me and really date me, then as a gentleman you play your part and be a man.

Within a year of closing Oxi Clothing, I was looking to buy property again. With the help of my parents scouting around for a place, we found a beautiful second-level, one-bedroom unit in Canterbury with a courtyard. At the time, I was dating a guy whose brother was a broker. Like I always say, people come into your life for a reason. Because I was single and earning an average wage, it was hard to get a loan. With the help of this guy I ended up buying my property, which was only five years old. I had a bit of saving after paying off my debts with Oxi Clothing and it was just what I needed.

As usual, I had a lot of so-called 'friends' saying that where I bought was a bit of an average area – though I am having the last laugh now, as the area has had a six percent increase in property prices and the development that has happened in Canterbury took off in 2016, with all the buses and train stations at my doorstep and being only twelve kilometres away from the city.

I also had the same thing happen when I bought in Arthur Street in Merrylands. The street had a few housing commission units opposite to where I lived and by 2009, I sold the property for a lot more than when I bought it. I had it on the market in 2007, though I took it off knowing I was not getting what I wanted. The real estate agent at the time thought I was clueless and, maybe because I was a single woman, kept pushing me to sell and told me that I would not get any more for this. Well, I went with my gut feeling and took it off the market and waited two years for it to sell at the price I wanted. Patience sometimes pays off.

With all the things going on in my life, I needed a break. One day I just clicked and got off all the dating sites and gave myself a break and focused on just me again. I meditated and kept myself healthy, even though for the last few years I had been struggling with chronic fatigue and I just didn't know why. I worked hard, as always, and was given six more stores to look after, I was the regional manager for twelve stores. As the six stores I had were making budget under my management, the staff I had now under my management went from forty to sixty, with no pay rises. My workload went through the roof.

It was when I was not putting it out there and was just focusing on myself that I met my future husband through a chance meeting.

'We don't meet people by accident.
They are meant to cross our paths for a reason.'

— Kathryn Perez

Meeting My Future

'You are my friend, my love, you make the best of me.'

— Unknown

I was lying in bed trying to decide whether I would go to the NSW state titles for boxing in 2011. I'd had such a massive week with working sixty hours, but a voice kept saying, 'Up you get and go and help the gym sell tickets for entry at the Fisherman's Club in Rockdale'.

I managed to get myself together and head down to the all-day event. It was a great day, filled with boxers, trainers and supporters, and here I was at the door, getting a glimpse of our boxers fighting while selling tickets.

I noticed a gentleman walk past me and out the door to get money at the ATM and come back. One of the ladies at the desk refused him coming back in. I stood up and mentioned that he was here from the morning and the gentleman replied that he was actually fighting this afternoon and thanked me for backing him up. I really didn't think much of it and resumed my business.

He came past a few times, looking at me as he walked past. I thought he was wearing the floor down, with the amount of times he walked back and forth. Was this guy fighting, or was he burning his energy, by wanting me to chat to him? I was egged on by the ladies at the desk and told that he might be interested. Well, he really was not my type. But what was my type? I had to think outside the box and keep an open mind. I went to get a glass of water at the bar and there he was again. He looked over with a big smile, and said, 'Hello.'

The hello was not just an ordinary 'hello': it really grabbed my attention. I introduced myself.

'Ken's the name,' he said as he kept smiling at me, then walked off back to his team.

I went back and told the ladies at the desk about the man that was wearing out the floor. Smiles were all around the desk: I was actually blushing. By the end of the day, Ken came up to me and asked me straight out whether I was married or seeing someone.

'No, I am not attached to anyone at the moment.' I had all eyes on me, even the boys from the gym were watching this all unfold in front of them.

'Great, I must be very lucky today! May I have your number so I can take you out on a date?'

I froze for a little bit, knowing everyone was watching, and, just like that, I gave Ken my number.

Ken was your true blue, fair dinkum Aussie bloke. He was older than me, which was good because after dating so many younger guys, I thought it was time to date someone older than me for once.

Within a few hours, I got a text from Ken. I was heading out to meet a friend for dinner and he was out in the city with his teammates. He was egged on by his mates to make sure he was given the right number. He knew deep down I had, though, his mates wanted to make sure it was not a fake. I replied back and eased everybody's minds.

Our first date was set a week after I meet him; he pulled up on his Harley-Davidson and waited for me to come down. It was a great date; we ended up in Cronulla for Thai food and then went across to Northies for a drink, where I ran into my workmates (of all the places!), then we went to the city to end the night with a hot chocolate at the Rocks. He dropped me off and I tested him, by inviting him up to the unit. He refused, like a gentleman, and said his goodnight then took off.

I had such a great night. It was relaxed and we had so much in common. He reminded me of Samuel, though on a more mature level, as he was older. He was into boxing and I admired that, as he was in his mid-forties and still training and fighting. His extended family are still in boxing. He was happy and supported the fact that I was a boxing coach at the Kostya Boxing Academy – at the time, he was at a boxing gym in Cabramatta. I had finally met a guy who accepted me, as a strong woman who used her strength in a loving way. I had no need to rely on Ken: I had my independence, my own wings to fly, and no-one was going to clip them and he could see that.

I organised a trip to go to Vietnam for two weeks with a friend. A lot of his friends thought it was wrong that I was going on my own without him, though Ken knew it wasn't a problem. So what if I was with him but wanted to go and explore with my friend? Ken was everything I wanted in a partner: he didn't care if I had a weekend away with girlfriends, went out with girlfriends, or even occasionally went out to dance parties. Ken was fine with it because he was secure within himself. A woman should never change and lose sight of herself and her independence. As a couple, you have to have some time to yourself.

Before I went to Vietnam, and three months into our relationship, Ken asked me to marry him. I accepted; I had nothing to lose. Life is short and you've got take those risks. Though my dad was not happy: my family thought I was going to marry a biker, as he had tattoos on his arms and rode a Harley. Although I convinced my whole family that Ken was safe, I guess they were just worried after the dramas I'd had in the past.

Ken came over and, as an old-fashioned guy, asked my father for my hand in marriage. Dad came out and said he was not happy with us jumping into marriage. This is the same father who before I met Ken encouraged me to be a single mum because I wanted a baby and was not getting any younger. Now that I had met someone and it was really happening, it was a no. He also did not want me marrying someone who had a child and Ken had a fourteen-year-old daughter from a previous relationship. Realistically, we all have baggage, and when you're in your thirties most people have kids and by the time you're in your forties, some have been divorced. Ken stood up to my dad, after I had to go for a drive to get lunch for the family. When I walked in, my face was white and Ken could see that I had had a mouthful from Dad. Ken told Dad how it was. Before you knew it, my mother randomly popped open a champagne bottle to celebrate. For my official engagement to Ken, he took me back to where we had our first date: out to a Thai restaurant in Cronulla and then to the Opera House, where he slipped my ring on, with the background of the beautiful Sydney Harbour.

Would you believe that my father ended up bonding with Ken over a plant? My father is a green thumb and loves his garden, and Ken also knew a thing or two about plants. Someone had given Dad a rhubarb to plant in his yard, but it was new to him and my father knew nothing about it. Just like that, the barriers came down.

I left for Vietnam for two weeks and in that time Ken had a boxing match, which he won. I also organised to get my wedding dress made in Vietnam; Ken gave me the idea of making it there. It was a great idea and the dress came out beautifully.

When I arrived back, I was still feeling the chronic fatigue and it started to play on my mind. My weight had fluctuated, even with me training and eating right. I put it down to a burn out. Ken could see that my job was taking a toll on my private life. It was really bad; I had to take figures for stores – even on my days off – three times a day: morning, afternoon and night, and that took an hour. Management didn't care if we were at a function, it had to be done. There were a few times it was even embarrassing: I had to do this at a wedding and at a birthday party. I needed to do something and eventually, after a year, I handed in my resignation. My health and having a work–life balance was important.

Ken moved in with me and by August 2011, Ken asked one of the sales managers from his work if there was a job available for me. It was a major logistics company. I had an interview as an account manager selling logistics. I was interviewed by two managers, and within two weeks I got the job. I didn't know a thing about logistics and selling services to small or medium-sized businesses. This was going to be a challenge, and for sure it was. I was in a male-dominated world again, surrounded by men in a logistics company. Women were not in logistics as much as they are now. I was allocated the areas of Wetherill Park and surrounds. I was thrown to the wolves; I could either sink or swim, and I was not going to sink.

I learnt my products and went out with various representatives to see the selling style; I even met up with drivers and found out about different companies in the area. It was very hard. Customers will either like you or dislike you, and at the same time you are selling a product, you are also selling yourself, as you are the front line of the company. I put up with a lot of ignorant men and even yelling from some – the way that some treated you … I was about to quit my job when my sales manager said,

'Silvana, you are a boxing coach outside of here, aren't you? How do you conduct your class? Treat selling in logistics like boxing and be a bit tougher with the clients and do not allow them to walk over you. They are testing you.'

She was right; I was treating my clients with too much customer service and not treating them like in business mode. I thought back to when I had the shop and how I managed in my last job. With all that onboard, my style changed really quickly and I was starting to see results. I realised that if I could sell logistics, I could sell anything.

My time at the logistics company was not easy; I was bullied by some of the team members and some felt, I guess, threatened. It's hard when you have questions and you want to do well for yourself and your company. I had come from fashion straight to logistics. Ken could see what was happening and wanted to do something, though I didn't allow him to intervene. I stayed quiet while I was put on the outer – mind you, it was all women in my team and sometimes that could be a very bad thing, with different personalities flying everywhere. Females can get so nasty, if things are not going right for them. Though it lasted for a year, I remained quiet. I guess my angel listened to me and the girls all left, whether by promotion or getting new jobs. I was the only one left standing when I came back from holidays.

On 19 February 2012 – exactly a year after I met Ken – we got married. Thirty-six people came, including family, and it was held at Birkenhead Point with a female celebrant, and then just a short walk to a café for the wedding luncheon. It was something different and the guests loved it.

The next day, Ken and I flew to Borneo for our honeymoon. Ken had never travelled abroad before and well, being married to me, I was going to open his eyes to a whole different world. I enjoyed watching my husband's face as he experienced being overseas for the first time. We were able to ride horses and watched the South China Sea. It was such an amazing trip. We saw so much history and although quad-biking through the jungles of Borneo was fun, the best part was staying at Shangrila, where they had a reservation for orphaned orangutans. People from all over the world came to the hotel to see these orangutans. We were told to stay back and one of the guides gave me a baby's bottle with orange juice in it. Before you knew it, a two-year-old orangutan came down and grabbed my leg. I looked down and gave her the bottle with juice; she held my hand until she had finished it. She realised that Ken and I were a couple and crawled up to Ken and hugged him, grabbing my head and his and holding us three together. We were both touched by what happened; even the guides were surprised. It was a moment we both will never forget.

'The things you take for granted
Someone else is praying for.

Be thankful.'

Wedding day

Health Challenges Keep Coming

'We don't grow when things are easy; we grow when we face challenges.'

— Unknown

Sitting on the couch during the only night Ken I had together without working or commitments getting in the way, we were watching *A Current Affair* and a report came on about PIP implants and symptoms. It sounded like something I'd had for years. My sister called as she was watching the show also. She begged for me to get a mammogram done, as the Australian government was offering free screening.

PIP breast implants are medical devices manufactured by a French company, Poly Implant Prothese PIP), which are composed of a silicone outer shell filled with a silicone gel. They were used in **Australia** from September 1999 until April 2010, before being recalled due to advice from the French regulator because they contained unapproved materials that may not have been safe.

I organised to get my breasts checked. My right implant had ruptured, though my breast looked the same. It was a massive case unfolding, as thousands of women from around the world were affected by this. In 2012, I went back to the doctor in Woollahra who had implanted mine in 2004. He had a dozen or more cases but because my records with the clinic were old, he decided that he would operate on me for free and the implants would be free, as I had private insurance. Many women did not have that option and had to pay thousands of dollars to replace the implants. Within the month, my implants were removed, but I also had a lump under my right armpit the size of a golf ball; the silicon had leaked into my lymph nodes and my lymph nodes had to be removed, along with the silicone. The silicone had leaked in my body, which explained why for years I had struggled with chronic fatigue.

I was implanted with a new set of implants and recovered well. Mind you, I was still working full-time and still making sales targets at the logistics company, and Ken, who I encouraged to get his boxing coach license (and did), was now taking my classes when I needed help.

In November 2013, I got a normal check-up with a pap smear and my results came back as positive, again. I could not take this anymore. What was happening with my body? I kept fit, even when my body wanted to stop, and I ate healthy. I was working full-time and teaching and believed that my body wanted to rest, and I was not listening.

The doctor mentioned that if I kept going with operations on my cervix, it was going to be taken out, as it would keep weakening and I would always have a problem. I wanted a child; having children was important to me, as the opportunities had been taken away from me in the past. I could not have this taken away from me again. I was forty-one years old and this was now the third operation on my cervix. He said that the virus was coming back, as my immune system was down and that it happens when you are doing too much and are stressed. He looked at me and said that I needed to slow down.

I was operated on again in November and I felt horrible. I could not train, Ken was teaching my classes, and despite my challenges, I kept on top of my work and kept bringing in the figures. When I went back to boxing, I never really told anyone what I was going through. I wanted to give it my best shot, even though there were evenings that I looked white and some of my clients were wondering what was going on with my health.

In February 2014, my world came crumbling down. I was at a sales conference in the city, staying there over night with eighty other employees. I had only had one or two drinks the night before and the next day we were gathered, talking about cases of bringing new clients on board, and I was speaking. Then something came over me, my speech started to slur and the left side of my face went numb, down to my left arm. I knew what was happening; as a boxing a coach and knowing about health and fitness, I knew I was starting to have a stroke.

Sitting outside, I had HR and my manager come out and ask what was going on. When I mentioned that I thought I was having a stroke, my manager laughed in disbelief. I didn't want the ambulance coming because I was stubborn, and because of their reaction I caught a cab all the way to Dulwich Hill. My GP had examined me, and without talking any further called 000.

'Silvana, you're either having a heart attack or a stroke. I cannot believe you caught a cab here.'

I looked at her. 'Doctor, I just didn't want it to be a false alarm.'

She shook her head and the ambulance was on the scene within five minutes. In the ambulance one of the paramedics took my blood pressure and mentioned she had never seen a reading so high. I felt I was going to explode.

Why was this happening to me?

I was rushed to RPA Hospital emergency and stayed there for three days. My parents found out that evening, but I didn't want anyone to worry about me. I was embarrassed that at forty-one years old, I was sitting in a stroke ward with four other men – some who could not even talk and were groaning. I hated hearing their pain. There were no beds or other rooms to go into. I felt uncomfortable being in a room with men that were all suffering from the effects of a stroke.

The nurses were greatly surprised that someone as fit looking as me was sitting in a stroke ward. Some explained that a stroke can hit anyone at any age. Before you knew it, there was a twenty-five-year-old wheeled in and placed on the bed beside me. All I could see was the family crying: he was a vegetable. I asked the nurse to close the curtain for me, as it was getting all too much. The nurse mentioned how lucky I was, that the scans could not see a blood spot on my brain, and that my fitness had played a major role for why I had recovered so quickly without any symptoms.

'Your training has saved you, for the recovery you needed. Do you have a heavy workload? Because stress is a big factor with stroke. Maybe this is a wake-up call for you.'

The nurse was injecting a drug called Clexane in my leg. I looked at her and thought about a few things that could have contributed to me ending up there. I thought about it even as the doctor was questioning my home life and work; he mentioned that if I kept going like this for years that it would catch up with me. My own mother kept warning me that I was not getting younger and that I needed to slow down. At that time, I was the breadwinner, as my husband had lost his job and it would be months before he could get a job again. I kept all this bottled up and it came out in my health.

Everything went through my mind, and also that I wanted to have a child, although Ken had had a vasectomy because he thought he would never meet anyone or have children again. I was determined; this was my dream and something I was going to do with or without him.

I was out of hospital and the conclusion was that they could not explain what had happened to me and that it could show up later in my brain with a blood spot. I went back to work after two weeks: yes, I was a stubborn person. I started getting back into training and work and spoke to Ken about having a baby.

'I am leaving this too late, it's now that I should try or never.'

Ken was all for it, knowing we had a challenge with him having been 'snipped'; the only way of doing this was through IVF.

People cross your path for a reason, I met a lady when I went to a meditation retreat at Box Hill a year ago and she explained how she was single and had tried IVF five times at the RPA, as she was a nurse there. I never knew that the RPA did this for half the cost of other hospitals and remembered having the conversation; I started to do my homework about IVF. Ken and I did all our tests to make sure that we were both healthy and our reproductive systems were in good shape.

My parents were worried about me trying for a baby, as I had gone through so much in recent years with my health. My obstetrician wanted my dream to come true though between him and my GP I had a great team of medical professionals to look after my needs for having a baby.

I booked the IVF appointment, which would be held in October 2014 – on a six-month waiting list. This was fine with me, as I wanted to be stronger and better for the next chapter of my life. In that time, I joined a commercial agency to get into TV and catalogue work, and to keep my mind active in a different field.

By November 2014, as I had to do pap smears every six months, I came up with being positive again. I could not believe this. How much more can a person take? And I was in the middle of IVF.

It had been such a challenging journey with my health in the last few years, though I reminded myself that there were other people that were less fortunate than me.

My obstetrician mentioned that he had never seen someone who'd had their cervix operated on four times. I knew now that this was going to be a miracle for me to keep the baby, as I had an incompetent cervix; but I was not going to give up. I am a fighting spirit and my doctor was determined, like me, to do his best to help me keep the pregnancy.

IVF had to be put on hold for four months until my pap smear was a negative response. I worked and trained myself to keep me going and keep positive.

I managed for three years to exceed new business budget figures and management was amazed at how I was able to keep above every new business budget. Work knew what I was facing with my health issues, though no-one knew I was facing an IVF challenge.

'Life is like a boxing match:
Defeat is declared not
When you fall,
But when you refuse
To stand again.'

— MUHAMMAD ALI

Ancient ruins at Angkor Wat, Cambodia

Looking Back: Fulfilling My Bucket List

'You will never find time for anything. If you want time you must make it.'

— Charles Buxton

While I continued with my life and waited to get the all clear for resuming IVF, I meditated on the past, present and future. I had come a long way and achieved so much during my life's experience to date. It was like I was ticking off my bucket list – and maybe I was, subconsciously. I thought about the small messages and the people I had met along the way that were encouraging me to live my life to the fullest, throughout my years.

My relationship with my father had been damaged for so many years. However, I am forever grateful that he was tough on me: it encouraged me to take the stance against him and do what my soul and heart wanted to do. He saw himself in me and realised that he had raised a strong woman well. From all that, I had paved the way for my siblings to go and explore what life had to offer. Things were made easier for them, as I had broken the mould and softened my father. Yes, I was the black sheep of the family and I never regretted anything that I did – even the setbacks of what happened to me. They had happened; instead of crawling into a corner and being a victim, I took a stance on my own and claimed my life back to achieve the things I wanted. Life is not about going out there and just making money: life is filled with a wealth of experience. How many people do you know that have gone out, taken risks and done the things they want, without caring what people say?

Only a handful.

Sometimes I think I really do not belong or I am not on the same page as my peers – or I have a conversation with someone and wonder where they picked up their brains from and it leaves me scratching my head. We all go through that moment, when someone does something and says something that is not right. I kept quiet with people like that and realised later, when I was older, that I was not going to keep quiet anymore. I was going to speak out and make a stance not just for me but for the others along the way that were frightened or bullied. There is nothing wrong with being powerful in a loving way and I believe the journey that I have gone through allowed me to discover aspects of myself I never knew; feelings that I thought I'd never had.

With all that in mind, my bucket list was being ticked off. I'm so grateful that I've been able to experience such amazing things all over the place, from when I was young with my parents and all the way through my life. I remember Dad taking us to different areas of NSW to explore this great land. I've also been camping with siblings and friends, though I hated camping – you always get that one person that snores or farts during the night …

In 2007 I had a crash course on how to scuba-dive from my brother who had scuba-dived more than 300 times. He gave me a suit that was three times bigger than me and I went diving into Shelly Beach at Manly. In the murky waters, I came face-to-face with a groper fish that was the same size as me. Funnily enough, after that he threw me into the swimming pool and showed me how to scuba-dive properly. I think it should have been the other way around! After that, I was able to go scuba-diving on the Great Barrier Reef.

I went to New Zealand in 2003 with my sister, who experienced being overseas for the first time and the highlight was both of us in a helicopter looking down on Queenstown and walking on the Fox Glacier. It was such a bond to have with my sister and exploring nature together.

In 2011, I trekked through the jungle of Vietnam with friends for ten hours to see a local tribe and stay with them overnight. We saw old man – who looked well over 100 years' old – smoking opium out of long pipe. He asked us if we wanted to smoke; I thanked him and said no. We even got buffalos charging at us, though we were saved by a lady in the village. The guide told us that our scent was something that the buffalos were not used to, and even some of the villagers had not seen Western people before.

We came across a group of school children and they followed us, holding hands all the way until they could not go with us any further. We got to the village covered in knee-high mud and slept on bamboo floors, where the huts were on stilts. It was such an experience living with a tribe so deep in the jungle.

One of my most precious and memorable trips was with my mother. It was my mission to take her out of her comfort zone. I remember taking her to explore a new country for the first time – the only other place she had been was Lebanon. In Langkawi, an island off Malaysia, we stayed in a bungalow overlooking the beach, and had monkeys coming down and visiting us every morning.

I even took Mum on a cable ride that was 700 feet above sea level and watched her panic and melt from the seat to the ground. She sat on the cable car floor, holding on for dear life. I should have filmed it, though she conquered her fear. I even got to explore seven Islands on a jet ski with two guides; I must have done 150 km on the jet skis, on open sea water and swimming in some amazing coves. This was just a dream – and to do this on my own, with only two guides, words still cannot explain the moment I was in. I saw the sea eagles, so many of them diving and eating from the boats that went past.

We went to the national park in Langkawi and swam with three-metre reef sharks, which made my mum start to panic again, when she saw their fins out of the water. All was safe, until leaving the island when I got separated from my mother, as there were different cruise companies there for the day. I saw my mother with one foot on the boat and the other on the stairs. I called out to her while the staff were trying to put her on board. My mother had no life jacket on.

That day had brought us even closer; my mother pulled back and looked at me. I ran down to grab her: it didn't feel right, as I watched the scuba-diving boat take off, overloaded on one side. A couple we had met from Denmark were waving at us when the boat flipped over and landed on top of people. My mum started screaming, and my first instinct was to dive in and rescue the children that were in the water. She begged me not to, and it was that begging that made me stop in my tracks. Before you knew it, other staff had dived in and other boats circled and got the ones that were trapped under the boat.

The greatest gift was having my mother there. I held on to her, as I knew we had both been looked after by the universe and God himself. I was able to help once I got on the main boat, as it was mainly from our boat that most of the people were injured. There were about ten people that needed medical attention; it was great that I had first aid training, as the captain and staff didn't know what to do. I had the Danish couple: the wife had water in her lungs, and an older gentleman in his seventies bleeding from the head. I had to act fast and made sure that I could grab water and towels from people that were on the boat, as the boat had no towels and we were running out of water. Some refused to give me anything and it showed me how low and selfish people can be. I yelled at some, as I had taken over from the captain and told them that I was here to help, as no-one else wanted to help the injured. I even had a mother refuse my help offered to her two daughters that were bleeding all the way from their stomach to their legs, due to having been pulled over and scraped by the barnacles on the boat.

I acted quickly and made sure that the ambulances were waiting at the main dock for the ones that needed attention first. I managed to calm everyone down as it was getting a bit hostile on the boat.

My mother looked at me and grabbed my hand and said that she was so proud of me for thinking so quickly on my feet. I was happy that my mother was sitting next to me: it changed our relationship and we became closer than ever. We both realised that it could have been a different story.

I asked her why she screamed the way she did, when I wanted to dive in and save people.

'I almost drowned when I was in my teens. I have never swum again after that.'

I understood. By the time we got to the dock, the injured were being taken to hospital. Most of them were staying at the resort that we were in. The management at the resort knew straight away what I had done and thanked me for doing something to help others. I got no thank you from the mother who I had tried to assist with her injured children, and I worked out that the older gentleman who was bleeding from the head was her father. I didn't expect anything: it's something you do for others. I have always been taught to help others in need and I will continue to do so without wanting anything in return. The only thank you I got was from the Danish couple, who I still keep in contact with today. They ended up taking us out to lunch and thanking me because the wife did have water in her lungs and I managed to pick that up and tell medical staff on arrival at the dock. She stayed in hospital until she got the all clear to leave.

My stay in Langkawi with my mother was extra special; we both loved our trip, despite the boat incident. You appreciated life even more when faced with something like that, and it opens your eyes to see that there are some very selfish people out there. But you must continue to do your bit in the world and make sure that you surround yourself with people that matter.

I travelled a lot with Ken after we were married. I promised him that every year we would visit places that we had not been to. We travelled to various locations around Australia, like Perth and Darwin. We also travelled for him to compete in Archery (Ken has won most of his tournaments), including, Kiama, Wagga Wagga and Orange, where most of his family are from.

Ken and I ended up doing the very thing we wanted to do in Koh Samui: training at the Muay Thai boxing camp. These boxers train for three hours in the morning and came back at night to do three hours again. All this to support their family and bring home food for them. I appreciated the boxers there; we managed to see a few fights and it just opened my eyes to see how young they were to be making a living. Ken did so well, training for three hours straight. We even got to meet some amazing people and celebrate our wedding anniversary at The Cliff, which was run by Australians and overlooked the beautiful coastline of the island.

In February 2015, we travelled to Cambodia into Siem Reap – what an amazing experience! We saw all the temples like Angkor Wat and Bayon, where the history was mind-blowing. It was also where collectively more than a million people were killed and buried by the Khmer Rouge regime, during its rule of the country from 1975 to 1979. Across the country, it wiped out almost a generation. It was sad, though it was a reminder of how lucky we are to be living in Australia. Ken and I were ever so grateful. I know I keep writing about how grateful I am, but we forget at times how good we have it. We should wake up in the morning and say thank you for what we have, as there are so many that have so much less and still manage to smile and carry on with their day.

While in Cambodia, we visited a village and did a cooking class – the money we paid went to the village to feed the families. Back at our hotel, Ken and I met a few staff members who would come and try to swim at dusk in the pool. We decided for three nights in a row that we would teach them to swim. We got such fulfilment in doing that, I felt so happy doing something that would help someone else.

For my fortieth birthday, we went to Hobart where my husband surprised me with a five-star dinner at the top of the revolving casino, enjoying the view at dusk.

These are just a few highlights from the places I have experienced. I remember them all so well and feel blessed that I got to get out there and explore and discover myself and what the world has to offer.

> 'Life is an experiment in which you may fail or succeed. Explore more, expect less.'
>
> —Santos Kalwar

IVF and Falling Pregnant: The Things Some Women Are Too Afraid to Voice

'I aspire
To be a giver;
A giver of love,
A giver of good vibes and
A giver of strength.'

— Unknown

By March of 2015, the doctor had given me the all clear for continuing with IVF. I had not told many friends that I was going through this because I had so many health issues that I had to deal with from the past. I was not sure if I could fall pregnant again; the last time had been with Brad and that was by accident and I didn't want everyone giving their advice on what I should be doing. IVF was stressful enough without everybody's opinions.

The doctors gave Ken and me a three percent chance of falling pregnant naturally, due to Ken having been 'snipped' for over eighteen years and because we were both over forty. But that was not going to stop us from trying. In August 2014 I started my injections of hormones to stimulate the development of follicles in my ovaries. I had to inject using a pen into my stomach each day and was also taking tablets and a nasal spray. I also had to have a blood thinning injection each day, Clexane, because I'd had a blood clot in the past. These were painful on some days; I would even look at the syringes for a while before I had the courage to inject myself.

It was a very difficult time and I really had to call upon my fighting spirit to continue on this journey. After two weeks, the hospital organised to remove sperm from Ken's testicles with a needle. He joked about it, though it was painful doing the procedure.

Then it was my turn. I was placed on a bed and the procedure to remove my eggs was not a pleasant one, as I felt the whole process. You could see the eggs being taken out on the monitors. It was over in fifteen minutes. I had thirteen eggs, which was an excellent result for someone my age. To fertilise them took a few days; I had three eggs that were good to use. This is an important step in IVF and my husband was over the moon – he kept calling us super humans.

With all this happening and me working full-time and coaching boxing, I had to stop with my training. I could not go so hard, exercising light was something I had to adjust to.

No-one tells you what you go through while doing IVF. It's hard on the body and the mind. I was a tough woman who had taken on so many challenges that had been thrown at me. Maybe it was all for preparing me to handle this.

Hardly anyone knew what I was going through. I worked and taught class and kept quiet about what was happening – only a couple of friends and my family knew, though I never spoke to them about what I was going through. It was hard: my hormones were everywhere and on top of that I was dealing with using Clexane for blood clots – another hurdle. My husband really didn't know what to do. He was working fourteen-hour nights, so I would hardly see him, and had to go to my appointments alone. I stayed strong and focused; I needed to be around people that were positive, as this played a huge role. I had to cut ties with a couple of friends as dealing with their dramas was too negative. They never asked how I was feeling or what I was going through. I really didn't care how long I had known them; I needed to be selfish for once and think about my own needs.

A week later, I experienced ovarian hyperstimulation syndrome (OHSS), which in my case was mild. I had a stomach that was the size of a six-month pregnant lady and the following day I had to have my embryos put in. I was assessed by the doctor at the hospital and was told that the transfer could not happen, due to the OHSS. It was too dangerous to put an embryo in. Yet again, I was faced with a challenge; my mother, who was with me, could see I was upset, though I remained calm and reminded myself that I had come this far and I was not going to stop. The drugs that I was taking for IVF had over-stimulated my ovaries and so I had to wait for a month before they could go ahead and do my first cycle of IVF. My embryos had to be frozen.

Some women going through IVF go through depression. I had to make sure that I was surrounding myself with positive things and people and began spending a lot of time with my nieces who always made me laugh.

In May 2015 I got the all clear to do the first round of IVF. It was so important for me to be around healthy people and to be careful about what I ate and to be observant about my surroundings. I had the transfer done and within a week I discovered a lump in my throat. I was still working full-time and thought it was just a sore throat. By the third day, I ended up with a massive lump growing on the right side. I went to my GP and tests were taken. Within a few days, the GP called me and said that I had cytomegalovirus (CMV), which is similar to glandular fever. How in the hell could I have picked that up? The doctor said that it could have been anywhere, that someone had coughed and I had breathed in the droplets of saliva. She knew about the embryo transfer and told me that I could lose the pregnancy. She mentioned that it was likely that the baby would come out deformed. I just sighed: really, this was getting worse. It was up to me to take medication, so I went home and thought about the actions that I wanted to take.

I took three weeks off work, as I was contagious, though luckily my husband had not gotten sick from being around me. I got worse and was rushed to RPA hospital. It took a while to see the doctor, and I had trouble breathing and the lump in my neck was getting bigger. I had the worst doctor, who thought I was making it up, until my husband had a go at him. He couldn't tell what was going on with me because he was young and inexperienced. It was such a bad experience.

I was sent home, but the next morning I had to have a doctor come to my house because I was having problems breathing, the lump was a size of a tennis ball and I had broken out in little water blisters all over my body. I told him that I had an embryo transfer and the doctor said that I needed to go to hospital immediately. We went back to the RPA and I told staff that I didn't want the same doctor; he was there and saw us and sheepishly looked away. I managed to get an older doctor who took all the necessary steps of analysing the blisters and my throat. After a few hours in emergency, he said that I had a virus that was like CMV and that I would need to go on antibiotics and I would lose the pregnancy. He told me that if I didn't take the medication, I would get worse and the only way to rid this was by taking medication.

Two weeks after that ordeal, I went to the RPA to get my pregnancy results. I had lost the pregnancy. It was disheartening – though looking back, maybe it was a blessing, as what had happened could have had an effect on the growth of the baby.

I was back at work and doing my normal duties. I was still doing really well with bringing in new business and excelling. I had to wait for another month before going through the second cycle of IVF. The hospital had to speak to me about maybe going this round naturally: no drugs. By this stage I had stopped my Clexane injections, and this time I had to time the transfer exactly, making sure that I didn't fall with my ovulation on a weekend, as the doctors didn't do transfers on the weekend.

So my transfer happened on a Friday and it went well. Within two weeks I got a phone call saying congratulations: I was pregnant. This was a little miracle; it was the right time. Ken and I had mixed emotions: happy and just surprised that I had fallen pregnant, without using any drugs to assist us.

My dreams of being a mother looked like they were finally come true. I notified my obstetrician and he was over the moon. This was the same doctor that looked after me with my previous surgeries on my cervix. I made the decision to stay with him, as he knew my history. I had the normal checks of blood tests and scans. I still trained at the local gym in the first trimester, though I had to change my routine a little bit.

In week ten, I had a blood test and scan that came back saying the little one had a larger neck for his growth at that week. I was booked in for a procedure at Sydney Ultrasound for Women in Camperdown to do CVS, which detects at one-hundred percent accuracy whether the baby has Down syndrome. My ratio was very high, at 1:19, and the doctor was concerned about the outcome. Ken and I were so upset and told each other to keep the faith and stay strong. The next day the test was done, using a very long needle that is inserted through the womb. I had one of the best doctors in town for this, and the reason why I say this is that a woman has a chance of having a miscarriage from this procedure, as the placenta fluid is taken out for testing. It felt weird, there was a bit of pain. I had to rest for the next three days with supervision, so Ken called work and advised of the emergency situation we were in. The procedure happened on Thursday, and Ken was back to work on Monday afternoon. During his shift he was asked to walk out: he was fired. My husband came home early and I knew.

'They have fired you on the grounds of your being a caregiver because of me. That's unfair! Ken you are taking this further to unfair dismissal.'

Ken did just that and took the relative action for unfair dismissal and his case went to a tribunal. Within two months of being fired, Ken had his case heard. He represented himself and it was done over a three-way conversation with his ex-employer and a commissioner over the phone. Although Ken's ex-employer thought they had won because Ken was representing himself, he was wrong; Ken won the case. Never undermine the underdog – it was a lesson that Ken's employer learnt hard. Ken managed to get casual work until he could find the full-time work he was looking for.

My test results also came back as all clear and I found out with that test that I was having a baby boy. Ken and I decided that his name would be Jacob: a very strong biblical name from the Old Testament meaning 'the holder of the heel', the supplanter. We both wanted a strong name for our little boy, as I had gone on a difficult journey with my Ken.

The doctor monitored me with visits every three weeks to his surgery, and I was told that I needed to be stitched, as I had an incompetent cervix that was shortening. I was admitted in week twenty-one of my pregnancy. My doctor came to see me the next day and told me that I could no longer train or even have sex anymore. It didn't bother me about the sex because of the way my body was changing – and don't forget that I was still injecting each day and taking Clexane and pessaries for my cervix to make sure baby Jacob and I were safe. It tested my relationship with Ken and, believe it or not, we became closer and got to know each other on a deep spiritual level. I discovered something else in our relationship: feelings came out that we both had never experienced before.

Our journey together through this rough time brought out a new side in both of us. Sex was not on my mind at all: I had to think about a new baby coming and I was going to do whatever it took to make sure that Jacob was safe and that I didn't have an early labour. Ken knew and felt the journey I was going through; he is an amazing person who understood my needs and put his on the backburner.

It took a lot of adjusting going from training four days a week to none. I struggled with putting on weight and my breasts getting bigger and sore. I went from a size 12C to a 16DD within a few months. I was in so much pain with my upper back that I had to see a physio three times a week to tape my upper back to keep me upright. The physio mentioned that most woman suffer lower back pain, but because my core was so strong from years of training I had all the weight at the front from my belly up which was throwing me off balance.

The next best thing to not training was to watch my eating, as I wanted to make sure that Jacob was getting the best nutrients possible. I frequently got asked if I had any weird cravings, and really it was pork and Slurpees, nothing else.

One day, at twenty-five weeks of pregnancy, I went to work in the morning and I had a leak. It was a concern and I called the nurse at the doctor's surgery. When I explained what had happened, I was told that I had to go to the nearest hospital straight away. So my co-worker had to take me to Canterbury Hospital Emergency. At first, they were not going to admit me as it was not my birthing unit, but as it was an emergency they finally allowed me in. My best friend of forty-three years came in to see me, as my mother was worried and could not make it. Michael came in and checked up on me, to give assurances to my mother that I was OK. My husband was notified at work and raced to be by my side. It was a tough journey and I reminded myself that I had to stay strong and determined.

I was told by my doctor that my driving had to be the bare minimal and that I had to stop driving for my job. I was made to only drive to and from work and now had a desk job. This frustrated me, as I am not the kind of person who can work at a desk all day.

At work, I had been given a trophy and was recognised for the most outstanding achievement: for consistently achieving and excelling the budget. Knowing the battle I had been through in the last four years, management recognised a determined fighting spirit who brought new business and was confident in closing the sales. This award was like my Ms Fitness Trophy, seeing those arms held up high. I did it despite the challenges; my work peers knew the struggle I was going through and were very supportive. I kept working and closing business deals, even from behind a desk.

I had also been nominated for account manager of the year. I didn't care that I didn't win; I was happy with my achievements. I remembered walking to the logistics company the first day and how naive I was, about how the company ran, and coming from fashion to logistics. Instead of walking out after being bullied, I grabbed my work by the horns and was selective with who I chose to let into my circle. I was the player, playing the game. I was able to read and handle every personality that I faced in my job; I took it like a boxing coach and treated it like I was in a ring waiting for the opponent to lay the first punch. That is how I won my business and how I had the confidence to come up against men who tried to intimidate me.

There was one logistics manager in particular who had it in for me. When I was moved from Wetherill Park to looking after areas of Silverwater and Homebush, he gave me a hard time and liked to test my knowledge and never was nice to me. So one day I selected him and a guest to attend the charity event for boxing. One of our fighters from the gym was fighting and this was being shown on GEM TV station. I put up my hand to host and knew I was the right person as I knew my boxing. Though I was not selected, I got a call the next day. It was the logistics manager on the phone. He was being really nice and I had to stop him and ask what was with the change in attitude. He apologised for how he had treated me over the previous two years.

'Silvana, why didn't you say that you were a boxing coach? All this time, you could have swiped me with a hook, upper and jab.'

'Of course I could have, though where is the fun of me being mysterious and knowing I was allowing you to win? How did you know I was a boxing coach?'

'The managers at the corporate box turned around and told me. I was in shock. Here I was judging a book by its cover.'

'Well they do call me the smiling assassin.'

From then on, he respected me; his attitude changed overnight. That was a perfect example of how boxing played such an important role in my life – and it still helps in every aspect of my life.

I explained to my managers, who asked how I did so well in the business, that I treated it like it was boxing: if I get hit and fall, I am going to get back up and keep throwing those punches and use strategy and be honest about the business I was dealing with of what I could and couldn't do for them. At the end of the day, you are the frontline and you are the face of the company.

I finished up work a week before Christmas 2015. I wanted to finish at the end of February 2016, though the doctor said it was not safe for me and the baby and I listened. He was worried about me because I was too active. He said doing things like housework and simply walking around the block would not be safe. He warned me that if I didn't listen to him, that he would hospitalise me until the birth of Jacob.

So what the hell was I going to do with my time? I ended up doing a course in personal training and I thought, I have two months to write my story. This was the time to write about my life and share my experience, before Jacob comes in the world.

On Holy Thursday, just before Easter, our miracle child arrived:
Jacob Ghoussain Thornberry.
Born 23 March 2016.

Here's to the next chapter of life!

Sea Change

'In the waves of change we find our true direction.'

— Unknown

It's not easy – hell no! I don't care what other mums say: it's hard caring for a newborn baby around the clock. I came from working two jobs, having a fast lifestyle, being out and about and getting rest and waking up whenever I wanted.

I struggled with looking after Jacob. People kept telling me: your life will change, do you want this at your age?

You know what? This had been my decision, and the choice I wanted to make. It may have been a bit later in my life, though I experienced so many things and I have no regrets.

I lived!

And I will keep putting the bar up.

Ken, having had a child from a previous relationship, was my major support with Jacob and still is. Everything I was told about – reading everything in the books – got thrown out the window. I really took everything on board going with my gut feelings. Advice from others came in from every angle, as everybody has an opinion, though it might not even work with every mother and child. I learnt from mistakes through trial and error very quickly.

I ended up going back to work for three months full-time, while Jacob went to full-time day care at six months old. It was in November 2016 that I traded my BRZ sports car for a mummy's car. Oh, I missed my car, where I would feel free driving and being a revhead at times. But it was the change I had to make for the life I wanted to look after.

I also thought that it was time to put my apartment up for sale, as we were living in a one-bedroom apartment with Jacob in our bedroom.

My apartment sold a week before Christmas. I knew that living in Sydney, twelve kilometres from the city, wasn't a place I wanted

Jacob to grow up. In that year, we looked at various places, as far as Wollongong and the Blue Mountains, but nothing really captured our hearts. So when I sold the place, I had three months to really think about where I wanted the family to live. Ken and I decided to maybe look out of state.

In January 2017, we flew for the long weekend to the Gold Coast and organised to see eleven properties in just one-and-a-half days, with forty-degree heat and a one-year-old in tow. We did the unthinkable.

After those eleven properties, our real estate agent suggested we look at one that was not listed in a great location in Southport. So I made the call to view. Some of you might know that when you walk into a place, whether you're renting or buying, your gut tells you yes or no. Straight away mine said yes.

I decided that was it and to go ahead now with the process of buying and getting everything in place for settlement.

Crazy: I was to buy our home and make the sea change, quit our jobs and do the unthinkable with my husband and little man.

> 'Life is all about taking risks.
> If you never take a risk
> You will never achieve your dreams.'
>
> — Unknown

It was 7 April 2017 when we moved from Sydney to the Gold Coast. We had dramas with our vehicles getting there before us. The removalist moved us the day before, so our hotel and flights all had to be cancelled – and we couldn't get a refund, we just had to cop it on the chin and move forward with the challenges and deal with it as best we could.

It took us a few months to settle in and get used to the fact that we had no family on the Gold Coast. I started to feel a bit down because I couldn't find work even though I applied every day since before I'd moved. I was getting rejection after rejection. On top of that, I couldn't lose the weight from having Jacob and I started piling on more. I was stressed. I was used to working and training, and I didn't have either. I started having alcohol almost every night, which made me feel really mad about myself in the morning, because now there was someone else in the picture I had to look after. For a few months I had a few glasses of wine at night, then it became every couple of nights drinking a bottle to myself.

Just before Jacob turned one, he had surgery to get grommets put in his ears, so on top of everything else, Ken and I were dealing with Jacob's slight loss of hearing and having puss ooze out of his ears all the time. I was also dealing with going to the doctors every second day, seeing specialists and having test after test with Jacob. It started to affect me and Ken, as he was in and out of work and we were trying to keep our heads above water.

I know most would say it was crazy that both of us had quit our jobs to have a sea change but sometimes you've got take the risks in life to achieve your dreams. If it doesn't work out, at least you tried. I wasn't going to give up: I needed to refocus and have a different approach to how I was living.

Jacob

Fitness Journey Is Reborn

'Every morning, you have two choices: To sleep with your dreams, or wake up and chase them.'

— Carmelo Anthony

At the end of July my family and I walked into a gym. I told Ken that I was going to train and get back into something that really I should have taken further back in 2001; I was going to compete again in body building. I couldn't get work; I needed something to focus on, after my son was going through so much. We had only a little savings to get us through the drought of no work. My doctor mentioned to me that I shouldn't feel guilty about competing, and if anything it would help me get through what was happening to Jacob and deal with it better.

I reminded myself that I had to put me first. My GP wanted to make sure I was OK, and I guess in a way she knew I was a depressed, even though I didn't confirm it with her. I looked withdrawn and exhausted, with the little man always up, and it was taking its toll on Ken too.

I was recommended a trainer and within a few a weeks started my training with Jackson, who had a reputation of taking clients to competitions. Every week I would meet with him to measure my body fat and look at my diet: what foods were working and what was not. Like any trainer taking on a new client, he didn't know my mental state and how driven I get with wanting to reach that end goal. Having been a boxing coach myself for over ten years and the fact that I was a personal trainer all played a role now with my mental state and where I was going.

I became focused and watched myself take shape. I saw things and did things that most people don't experience in their lifetime. I told myself that I would surround myself with people that were positive and uplifting and had the same values as me. I believe what you put out comes back to you.

My mind was not able to cope with my son suddenly being in

hospital again, in August 2017. My mum was on the way here from Sydney, as emergency staff worked to get Jacob stabilised. They said he had MSRA and my husband and I asked what the hell was that? My son had been in hospital in March that year for his grommets, and now this?

It turned out that he had a specific staphylococcus aureus (staph) bacteria that is resistant to most antibiotic treatments, called the superbug or Golden Staph. How did Jacob get this? From anywhere: mainly from playgrounds and where there are a lot of people in one area. My poor son going through this ... he was a real fighter; I could see in his eyes that he was fighting this. Our son was hospitalised for five days and isolated from other patients. Hospital staff came in, all caped-up, as this was a serious infection. I stayed there while I was prepping for my figure competition, which was in October 2017. I stayed five days in hospital with my son and my mum by my side while Ken was at work.

Jacob fought the infection, with the help of the great staff at the Gold Coast Hospital, and we were back on track for a while and I was able to enjoy my mum being there.

The day came in October when I was to compete. I competed in Figure across five categories for ICN Federation and was accompanied by my trainer and posing coach, along with my husband and Jacob, who had taken the spotlight and was interviewed by the presenter from ICN.

I walked away as a winner – not with a medal or being placed, but the fact I finished my goal to compete. I was happy and proud about how I was looking. All the hard work and determination had paid off and my husband was there to see me making my comeback.

I learnt a lot from that competition; only do two categories, as I almost collapsed by the end of the day, by doing five. You've got to look dry and have minimal water and certain foods to eat in order to come in looking lean and make sure all your muscles are showing. People don't realise what goes into preparing for a competition: it's not an overnight thing and it takes months. It took me four months to get into shape, losing 16kgs to make it on to that stage.

I walked away, and my Facebook page flooded with congratulations as I posted the amazing outcome of my fitness journey for the many friends that followed me.

I thought I was done from competing, but my fitness journey was just starting. I wanted to show other mums and dads that with little steps, you can reach your end goal. You have to take time out and look after yourself; if you don't, how are you going to be productive for the rest of your loved ones? I wanted my son to know that Mummy and Daddy are active and enjoy having a healthy lifestyle. I know it gets hard, with bills, working, household chores and kids' activities – but you've got to make time for yourself, even half an hour or ten minutes for that day.

I changed trainers and decided to go with a female. I felt it was the right fit for me, as she had a better understanding of how my body and hormones worked. It's funny: I had actually met my new coach a few months earlier, when she did my bikini for my October competition.

Mandy Butler was former Ms Australia for WFF in 2012 and took me on board. My next goal was ANB Federation for the Darling Downs Classic in May 2018 in Toowoomba.

While I was training and dieting, I had another challenge: my son had surgery on his ears, getting the grommets and nodules taken out; and my husband was bitten by a white-tailed spider on the back of his right knee. He went into emergency and had to have surgery, which put him out for two months. Financially we were not doing well, and I was also trying to find money to fund my competition. Mandy helped in any way she could, and I became sponsored by her business, Pro Stage Wear.

It was taking a toll on me; I was pushing myself with the stress of competition, finances and my family being ill. I know some might say I was selfish doing the competition when my family needed me, but the competition and preparing for it saved me mentally. There were times I wanted to walk away from everything and just disappear; my thoughts started to get dark. Then I reminded myself, when I looked at pictures of my last competition and my family, that I needed to hold it together for my son and my husband.

'Never give up, for that is just the place and time that the tide will change.'

— Harriet Beecher Stowe

I placed second in Figure at the ANB Federation. Happy with my outcome, Mandy suggested that I should try WFF Federation, as I had a shape for Figure performance. I really just wanted to rest, though I believed I had it in me to keep going, as it was only a month away.

Mandy decided that I would meet up with her and she would introduce me to Victor, who was the promoter for the shows in Queensland. We met one afternoon in a gym in Southport. I was definitely a Figure girl and was told that I would go well in performance because I looked lean for a Figure girl. Weight had to be around fifty to fifty-five kilos with height above 165 centimetres.

The Southern Hemisphere competition had come around really quickly and before you knew it, in May 2018 I placed second in Figure performance and qualified to go to Singapore. I had said to Mandy that if I placed, I wanted to take the opportunity to go and represent Australia for WFF.

I was taken on board to represent Australia for WFF Australia. I told the news to my husband and my family back home in Sydney, I was still in disbelief that I was going to Singapore.

In Singapore I shared a room with Jessica, a woman who in her own right had been successful competing in fitness sports for four years and lifting weights for eight, now had made the change over to Figure. Jessica had won Miss Southern Hemisphere and was now in Singapore with me. We experienced a lot leading into the competition.

One of the memories I will never forget was weigh-in day before the competition. I stripped down to only my undies to make weigh-in and Jessica took off the clip in my hair – even that made a difference by 0.25 grams. I made my weight right on fifty-five kilos. I had to lose four kilograms in four days and I cannot believe how I did it. A lot of water loading: eight litres each day for two days. Thanks to the help of Superwoman Jessica.

The day had come, 1 July 2018, where the event was held at Zouk Nightclub. There were 300 athletes from around the world competing across all divisions, from body building to bikini models. Here I was in disbelief: the time for me had come around so quickly and before you knew it, I was standing in front of fifteen international WFF judges and waiting for the placing to be called out.

'Second place Ms Figure Performance, Silvana Ghoussain, Australia.'

I stood there not registering for a split second. *What just happened? I've been placed?* I couldn't believe the dream had been lived. I did it. I took the risk and went out of my comfort zone, thinking I was not good enough to be amongst these athletes. This moment proved to me that success can come in different shapes. On this day, I did something right, to be placed for my first international event.

I was excited, and at the same time different emotions started to engulf me. My past flashed before me as I stood on the stage. All the rough times I had been through and the strength I showed in those times hit me. I had done it. I had followed through with a dream that fell out of my hands in 2001. I had come back stronger and showed that we all have different journeys to go through to be standing on that stage. Mine was all that I thought about: my life journey had come in full force in front of my eyes, as I bowed down to take the medal around my neck. The silver shined, and it reminded me of what I have overcome time and time again in my life.

Back in Australia, on 30 September, I competed for WFF QLD titles and came in second place. This preparation was the hardest. I had so much going on, with working full-time and my marriage almost falling apart, along with battling bulimia. Not everyone is built the same and I realised the damage I was doing to myself physically and mentally. The effect was showing on my family. I wasn't in the best condition to go on that stage; I had put so much pressure on myself because of my results in Singapore. I felt like I couldn't get my energy back.

But no matter what the trainers said or did to help, no-one knew the hardship I was going through. I wanted to finish and not quit, no matter how I was looking.

I sought professional help a few days before my competition from doctors and dietitians when I recognised the fact that I had an eating disorder and that it was out of control. I knew something had to change; I decided that Figure was not for me and that I needed to change everything, including trainers and gym, and sort myself out to get back on track to be present with my family. They had been nothing but a support system that was unbreakable. My husband proved he was my ultimate strength and my rock. I made a decision for the coming year to compete in a different federation. On the 11th May 2019, I competed in the WBFF on the Gold Coast, Australia. This competition preparation was not about placing, which I didn't. Rather, I wanted to transform myself by entering a bikini division. I wanted to take myself out of my comfort zone and conquer a fear, which I did by entering a massive fitness federation. I wanted to show what body transformation has done for me, not only physically but also mentally.

I never gave up: I found an alternative and help when I needed it. The old Silvana would have gone on her own and kept going till she would have fallen over or burnt out. Now, I recognised that what was happening was affecting the people I love. Nothing is so important in life that you cannot find an alternative way to achieve your end goal. I felt my journey as a Figure competitor had reached its end path and I felt it in my heart. I had done everything and more in 2018, beyond my expectations. I knew that the change had to come, for my own wellbeing. I had set out on my fitness journey and conquered myself.

I am looking forward to what the future brings; I am forever evolving and looking forward to creating a better version of myself.

I am a force: the lioness who slept for a while has waited for that moment to rise and fight for what she so believes – that moment was right this minute.

In my own right I celebrated the lioness arising. I had awoken and realised that my husband had given me the greatest gift: to go and live my dream. I did my family proud and the congratulations flooded in. I was humbled, and it has taken great courage to make a difference to me and to anyone that has now followed my fitness journey in this short amazing year and a half. I want to be the person that inspires others, because I know the pain, the hurt and disappointment when things get really hard.

I know the haters will come; I know the people that are truly happy for you; I know the people that praise and want you to be successful on your journey. I know there are people who are negative. I learnt to choose carefully who I associate myself with. Something my father told me that will forever be embedded in my mind, is that you count the friends you have on one hand: choose them wisely.

This applies even more now that my son is in the picture: I have become the lioness who protects her young.

I celebrated with my husband and son back on the Gold Coast. Things started falling into place: I got a full-time job as a manager working for an active wear company, though it was not for me and I left after three months. I also found work with an agency for commercial TV. The doors have started to open up because I had competed.

I ended up being a semi-finalist as a cover girl for a fitness magazine in the December 2018 issue. I also waited for two months to have a fitness shoot at a very exclusive gym at the Mirana Mirage Resort. I had a met a lady some months beforehand when I had been for a job interview in Brisbane and she connected me with another lovely lady who happened to be an amazing photographer, who helped shape my profile through fitness shoots.

Life can take a different turn; it's up to you how you drive that journey. It's up to you to make that impact in your life. I have always been a fighter and one who tackles the challenges as they come.

I do believe that the universe works in mysterious ways. My journey has seen me accomplish many things that I put my heart into, even when the challenges kept coming. Even when I had obstacles and had people discouraging me in what I was doing. That gave me more drive to just go out there and get it.

Follow what you truly desire and don't let the challenges discourage you in any way. Yes, go after what you are passionate about.

Well, I've hit my fifties now with my beautiful son, who is following in his mum and dad's footsteps. It's funny how life comes back in full circle. In 2019, I moved back to Sydney. Even with COVID-19 and lockdowns, I kept going by competing again in bodybuilding, taking out a number of medals in my division. I even became Ms Sports Model, ICNNSW, 2020 for the over forty category. And in September 2022, I came back on board at the Tszyu Boxing Academy. Things happen when they are meant to happen.

A few weeks after getting back into boxing coaching, I competed for the first time in the Ms Fitness Australia in Sydney, NSW. I worked hard with my Coach GMF Team and set a goal in November 2021 to get my Professional Athlete Card at the age of fifty. On the 25th September 2022, I did just that—I became a Figure Pro Athlete. I worked hard, despite going through a lot of hormonal changes with menopause. I refused my GP's advice to go on hormone replacement therapy, as I wanted to use more natural remedies to ease my symptoms. To my advantage, it worked and I was able to make my dream a reality.

I'm here to show others that things can be achieved if you have the drive and put your mind into doing what you want in life. Life does not stop at a certain age. I feel more than ever I have so much to give, being in my fifties because I have experienced so much.

My quest is to keep being that mum who strives to show her son that if you want something, you need to go and chase that desired goal.

From a whisper to a roar, the lioness will keep being that fighting spirit.

Here's to the next unknown chapter of my life journey …

Professional Athlete Award, Ms Fitness Australia

Remember the Important Things In Life

'People inspire you, or they drain you;
Pick them wisely.'

HANS F. HANSEN

I had a few people ask why I want my life to be read by all, as our lives are usually a private matter. Am I doing the right thing by having my life as an open book? There is no right or wrong. I'm hoping that even in a small way, maybe I can inspire or motivate someone to seek help or to go out there and take that dream and make it a real-life thing. You have heard this plenty of times: that dreams can be made into reality and to go and achieve that goal. We can only achieve these things when our heart and mind are as one and we are happy within ourselves and have that fighting spirit to be determined enough to go out into the world and face it straight in the eyes.

Do not be afraid of failing in the things you do. By getting up and trying again, that is where success lies. Don't you think the people who have made it in whatever industry they are in haven't failed time and time again and have faced all the setbacks themselves? The one thing that they all have in common is the determination to get up and fight for what they believe in.

Do not be afraid to do something: everyone has an opinion and there are so many people out there who are negative and insecure about their own existence and of doing something and going for it. The amount of times I have had someone say to me, 'What about what people think?' Well, all can I say is, 'who cares what people think?' I would not have done half the things I had if I had listened to those people.

Life is about taking risks. You do not realise how short life is until you experience something traumatic, or a loss. We should not wait for this to happen to realise that there is more to life. We should be able to get out there and just do it.

Always surround yourself with people that have goals in life and are positive. When we surround ourselves with emotional vampires (as I call them: the ones that suck the life out of you) it can have such an effect on your life and you find yourself feeling negative about the smallest things. My journey has always been to help others and give advice and putting my needs last.

In the last few years, my attitude has changed and I have begun to look after my needs first. I started to see a change and stand up to people that are selfish and was able to speak my mind in a loving way. You should not have to tear yourself apart to keep others whole, and I had to learn that the hard way.

As my father said, 'As you get older, you count the number of true friends you have on one hand.' He was right.

Remember to aim at your goals: always start small, even if means writing them down, ask questions, and do your research. We are learning every day and it's amazing when you have a wealth of knowledge at your feet.

Wake up and say thank you for what you have around you. So many people in this world have hardly anything and still manage to smile.

Visualise what you really want and put it out there in the universe; you never know what opportunities will come at you. Never miss that door when it opens in front you.

Smile at strangers: you do not know what day they have had, and that could make a difference for them.

Take more time to heal old wounds and reconnect, especially with family; it's important to have that support system around you.

Be a fighting spirit and go after the things you want in life, whether it's family, making money, career or travel; just remember the important things in life.

Three Simple Rules in Life

1. If you do not go after what you want, you'll never have it.
2. If you do not ask, the answer will always be no.
3. If you do not step forward, you will always be in the same place.

— Nora Roberts

With My Son, Jacob

Transformation

At 50

SILVANA GHOUSSAIN MOTIVATIONAL SPEAKER

Book Silvana for your next speaking event.

When the challenges of life threw Silvana into a spin, she dug in and discovered her inner fighting spirit.

Be inspired by Silvana's story, and learn how to find your inner fighting spirit and triumph over adversity.

Contact Silvana Ghoussain
www.silvanaghoussain.com

www.ingramcontent.com/pod-product-compliance
Lightning Source LLC
LaVergne TN
LVHW051555070426
835507LV00021B/2587